FLORIDA FRESHWATER FISHING GUIDE

BY MAX BRANYON

A PUBLICATION OF THE ORLANDO SENTINEL

SENTINEL COMMUNICATIONS COMPANY

ORLANDO / 1987

Copyright © 1987 by Sentinel Communications Company
633 N. Orange Ave., Orlando, Fla. 32801

Edited by Dixie Kasper
Designed by Bill Henderson
Cover illustration by Larry Moore
Illustrations by Mike Wright and Brad Wegner
Back cover photograph by David Cotton
Text photographs courtesy of The Orlando Sentinel, Max Branyon and the
Florida Division of Tourism

Printed in the United States by R.R. Donnelley & Sons Co.

First Edition: July 1987

Library of Congress Cataloging-in Publication Data

Branyon, Max, 1931-
    Florida Freshwater Fishing Guide.
    Includes index.

    1. Fishing--Florida. 2. Fishes, Fresh-water--
    Florida. I. Title.
SH483.B73   1987   799.1'1'09759   87-13044
ISBN 0-941263-01-0

FLORIDA FRESHWATER
FISHING GUIDE

About the Author

Max Branyon writes the Fishing Forecast for *The Orlando Sentinel*. His column appears daily in the sports section. *Florida Freshwater Fishing Guide* is his third book. He is also the author of *Florida Boating and Water Sports Guide*, and a contributor to numerous outdoor publications.

His hobbies include fishing Florida's fresh and salt water for anything and everything from small, scrappy bluegills to 7 - foot sailfish and 10 - foot marlin. One of his favorite sports is going after Florida's line-busting largemouth bass — and he's caught many in the 10 - to 12-pound class.

He remembers the first fish he caught: "I was 5 years old when I caught a large shiner on a cane pole and a bent pin for a hook and a piece of wiggly earthworm for bait. I was so excited that I ran all the way home, my bare feet spanning the mile home in record time."

Max is a member of the Florida Outdoor Writers Association, the Outdoor Writers Association of America and the Southeastern Press Association. A former president of the Orange County Sportsmen's Association, he has won awards in fishing, outdoor writing, photography and conservation. His *Florida Boating and Water Sports Guide* won first place in the 1985 Florida Outdoor Writers Association annual competition.

———

Contents

List of illustrations

Acknowledgements

Special thanks to the Florida Game and Fresh
Water Fish Commission, especially to fisheries
biologists Jon Buntz and Kristen Storms and to
the regional offices' staff for their assistance.
Also, to the Florida Department of Natural
Resources, the National Marine Fisheries
Service, the Florida Division of Tourism, and to
my wife Donna and sons Steve, Bob, and Kyle,
who have all helped to make this book possible.

1

KNOW YOUR FISH

Moving to Central Florida 25 years ago was one of the best things that ever happened to me. I had yearned to live in Florida ever since the short time spent in the Panhandle during World War II when my dad was stationed at Camp Gordon Johnston near Carrabelle.

Those were some days.

As a youngster, I used to entertain myself by roaming the beaches and piers with a fishing rod and cut mullet or a few shrimp in hand. When dad arrived late in the afternoon, we'd load up our fishing poles and a can of worms and head for a couple of wilderness lakes. It wasn't unusual to take home stringers loaded with largemouth bass, shellcrackers, catfish and chain pickerel.

We could almost taste the sweet smell of those fish we were cleaning as we conjured visions of them sizzling to a golden brown in mom's large black skillet.

The next day we'd head for the Gulf of Mexico for some saltwater fishing — spotted sea trout, an occasional redfish, plenty of croakers and pinfish and lots of unwanted sea cats.

Some years later, as I stood ankle deep in snow looking over a frozen Chorwon Valley in Korea, I longed for the return of those days. The visions were still fresh in my mind — the old wooden skiff I kept down by the beach, the phosphorescent streaks of mullet in the surf at night, piercing the waves like artillery tracers, swimming in the surf, getting lost in the scrub searching for a hidden lake, and then wandering in circles for hours.

After I moved to the land of the largemouth bass, I became determined to catch one of those 10-pound lunkers. It might take me 10 years to do it, but I'd do it. As luck would have it, I caught two during the first year; but not before I'd almost given up in frustration.

Taking my dad's teasing advice to "quit using thread," I moved up from a 6-pound test monofilament to a 15-pound test — in desperation and against my principles at the time — and finally boated my first 10-pound bass. The thrill was as great as what I'd experienced as a boy when I caught my first bass, a 2-pounder in Big Lake Tucker near Carrabelle.

Now the biggest problem I have is trying to decide what kind of fishing I want to do next. Besides some of the best bass fishing in the country,

Florida also holds its own when it comes to bluegill, shellcracker and speckled perch. And then there are the saltwater species — snook, tarpon, sea trout, redfish, wahoo, marlin, sailfish and plenty of others that offer an angler a battle worth remembering.

Decide what kind of fishing you want to do and chances are you won't have to go very far in Florida to find it.

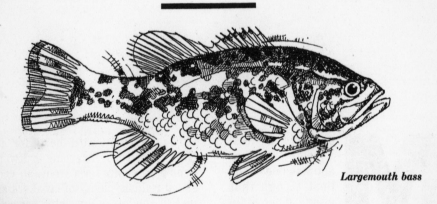

Largemouth bass

Florida's largemouth bass can be the dickens to please. You have to offer bait when it is hungry or make it angry enough to strike. Sometimes, if you can give your lure just the right twitch, a largemouth will strike out of instinct. Its dinner menu includes live shiners, shad, bugs, salamanders, snakes, crawfish and mice. It has been known to devour frogs and even ducklings. I've seen a lunker go after a redwing blackbird perched on a cat-tail.

Most lunker bass are females. The male rarely exceeds 5 pounds.

Not only is the largemouth bass the most popular freshwater game fish in Florida, the wily scrapper is the most sought-after game fish in the country. California is hoping to get into the game by importing the

fish into its lakes. What's everyone after? The glory of topping the world record of 22 pounds, 4 ounces. George Perry caught that one on June 2, 1932, in Georgia's Montgomery Lake.

Tim Stallings, an Orlando tackle shop operator, has a bass mounted on a shop wall that catches many a customer's eye. It is indeed a bass — a sea bass that weighed more than 30 pounds. With a little help from Ocoee taxidermist John Bartoletti, it looks like a freshwater world-record largemouth. And while the monster's not authentic, it gives Florida anglers something to dream about.

Bass are the largest species of the sunfish family. Colors vary from a silvery light green to a very dark blackish green. An isolated strain of largemouth is found in Florida lakes. Its fast growth rate, fighting nature and excellent taste combine to make it popular, according to the Florida Game and Fresh Water Fish Commission.

Florida's largemouth bass normally spawn in early spring in saucer-shaped depressions in the shallows of lakes, ponds and streams. The male is the scout; he selects the site, sweeps it clean with his fins, then waits for a female to join him in the reproductive ritual. After the female deposits the eggs, he fertilizes them. The male guards the eggs until they hatch and reach three-quarters of an inch in length.

If the fingerlings survive predators such as fish, birds and certain insects, they will attain a length of 8 to 10 inches and weigh about a half-pound by the time they're a year old. The yearling is sexually mature and ready to begin the reproductive process.

Largemouth bass prefer the cool of early morning or late evening to feed in the grassy shallows. Grassy areas also offer cover to the bass during non-feeding periods. Bass like to hang out around submerged trees. Other haunts include shelves, depressions, pilings, fishing docks, moored boats and almost any type of underwater structure.

Like people, bass seek shade and cooler temperatures when it gets hot. They head for cooler deeper water, shaded docks or grass cover. Night fishing is especially productive during the hot months. Daybreak and the first couple of hours after can also prove productive.

Bass head for deep water during extremely cold weather. A depth finder and a good selection of jigs and deep-running lures come in handy for cold-weather fishing. Many anglers use temperature gauges to help them find spots where bass may be. Free-lining a shiner may also entice a lunker.

HOW TO FISH FOR BASS

Live bait: Live shiners are responsible for catching more lunker bass than any other bait — live or artificial. Anglers serious about going after the real heavyweights use native shiners — those that come from the lake the angler plans to fish. Use bread for chum — a tiny hook baited with a doughball — and you can usually come up with your own native shiners. If this sounds too much like work, most local tackle shops or marinas have live imported shiners and some carry native shiners. Use a number 3/0, 4/0 or 5/0 hook through the shiner's lips or just underneath the dorsal fin near the tail. Some anglers prefer to free-line the shiner without a bobber (or cork) so that it can swim encumbered only by a hook, which looks more natural and gives it more depth range than a shiner with a bobber set at a certain depth.

Other fishermen like to use a bobber. Inexperienced anglers sometimes make the mistake of getting a bobber that is too big. The bobber (or cork) should be just large enough to hold up the hook, bait and sinker. If you use one, the sinker should be just heavy enough to take the bait down slowly and naturally. Sometimes a small split shot will do the trick.

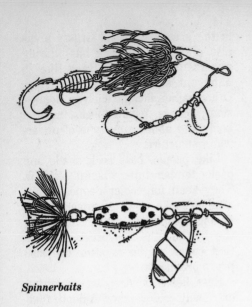

Spinnerbaits

Spinners: Lake fishing with spinners requires considerable thought and patience. Weedless spinners with a bucktail or pork rind are excellent to use in brushy shallows for bass. Generally, bass strike best at a slowly retrieved spinner, although there are times when they will smash a spinner gurgling rapidly over the surface. One of the most effective methods of fishing a spinner is casting it into deep water and letting it settle to the bottom, then slowly retrieving it up the side of a drop-off or a gravel bar. Other methods include trolling a spinner slowing behind your boat or canoe or casting a spinnerbait up on the shore and reeling it into the water from the shoreline to give it that natural look of a tasty morsel swimming into the water from shore.

Plastic lures: Plastic lures, especially the plastic worm, caused a revolution in bass fishing. For years manufacturers had made worms, minnows, crawfish and frogs from rubber. The fish showed some interest from time to time, but when the soft plastic lures hit the market, fishing results took a tremendous upswing. The plastic worm is the leader, with the

eel in second place. A flipping eel, which hit the Florida market in 1986, has become a popular item for those who use the flipping method of fishing.

Whether you plan to use a plastic worm or eel, the most popular rig is the Texas rig — a combination of a bullet lead and a 2/0 to 5/0 hook, which is barely run through the head of the worm and then back into the worm to make it weedless. Some fishermen impregnate the worm with various scents to attract the bass. Others insert a small plastic capsule with tiny lead balls as a noisemaker to attract the fish.

Use a Texas rig, a sharp No. 2/0 or 3/0 hook, and count to no more than three before setting the hook with an upward motion of your wrist. This method doesn't give the fish long enough to ball up the worm or drop it before you can set the hook.

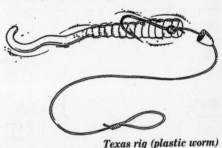

Texas rig (plastic worm)

Other plastic lures that emulate small shiners or shad, some with spinners attached, often take their share of bass as well. Work plastic lures slowly, especially worms and eels. Cast them into weeds, around shoreline docks or structures. Let them sink to the bottom and sit for a second or two before lifting your rod tip and letting the worm come up and then settle back to the bottom. The experts say you should repeat the process.

If the bass hits while the worm is on the way to the bottom or just as it reaches bottom, give a short hard jerk with the wrist to set the hook into the tough mouth, allowing you to release it unharmed. Otherwise, the bass may swallow the lure. If it does and you still want to release the fish, clip your line and leave hook and worm inside. The bass has a better chance of survival if you do. It is especially important to release bass during spawning season — the females are laden with roe and the bucks guard the nests.

Devil's Horse

Crankbaits and surface lures: Casting surface lures such as the Devil's Horse, Rapala, Bangolure, Bass Slayer and Zara Spook II along a grassy shoreline early in the morning is sure to bring results. Don't rush the retrieve. Often the bass will strike the lure while it's lying motionless. Many lures, such as the Rapala and the Shad Rap, lie on the surface until you start the retrieve. The faster you reel it in, the deeper the lure runs. Sometimes the fish will take it slow; other times they'll hit when you're retrieving it as fast as you can.

Deep-running Bomber lure

There are so many effective lures on the market today. It would be impossible to name them all, but a few good standbys are the Model A Bomber, the Rat-L-Trap, Deep Wee

R, Bagley Shad lures, Shad Raps and other Rapala lures, Hellbenders, Finn Mann and Big Os.

Rapala bass lure

A few of the favorite surface lures include the Zara Spook, Bangolure, Devil's Horse, Jitterbug, Bass Baffler, Griner plug, The Zara II, Rhoden's Baby Rattler and the Dalton Special. Some surface lures, such as the Zara Spook, are more effective when "walked" across the surface by upward jerks of the rod while moving the head of the lure from side to side. A topwater lure chugging rapidly and noisily across the calm water can drive a bass wild. Surface lures work best when the water is relatively calm.

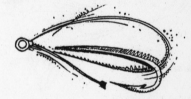

Silver Minnow spoon

Other effective bass-getters are spoons — Johnsons and Reflectos are among the best known. You can put a pork rind or a skirt on the spoon to make it even more tantalizing to a largemouth. One of my favorites for wading and grass fishing is a black Johnson spoon with a yellow skirt. This combination can be worked through the thick weeds with a slow retrieve for good results in Lake Tohopekaliga on the upper Kissimmee River Chain, but I get better results with a plastic worm when fishing the grass in Lake Okeechobee.

Jigging is an excellent way to

fish, especially when the bass are in deep water. Cast the jig to the bottom and give it up and down jerks for best action. Other jigs such as the Sassy Shad or Prissy Shad can be retrieved slowly to emulate a swimming shad, a favorite meal of the largemouth.

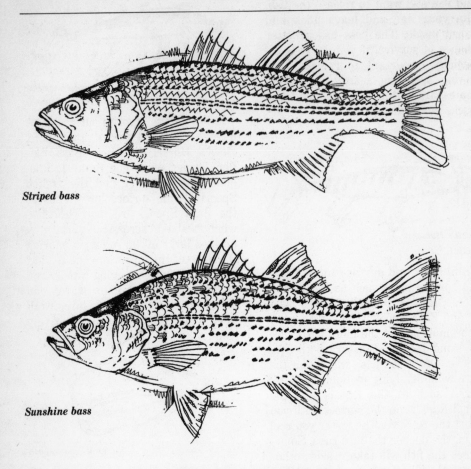

Striped bass

Sunshine bass

KINDS OF FISH

Striped bass and sunshine bass: Two of Florida's scrappiest fish are the striped bass and the sunshine bass (a cross between a white bass and a striped bass). Stripers and sunshine (hybrid) bass are cool-water fish by nature. Warm water makes them lethargic to the point that they refuse to exert the energy it takes to chase their prey. During the summer months, stripers and sunshine bass move into deeper water where it's cooler. You may find them in water as deep as 25 feet in late summer.

Early fall generates a reversal of this process, according to Tom Vaughn, chief of fisheries management at the Florida Game and Fresh Water Fish Commission. Colder air temperatures and cool surface waters bring the stripers and sunshines back up. Fishing activity for these two fighters really picks up when water temperatures drop to 65 to 70 degrees, Vaughn said.

These bass are open-water, roaming predators that like to hunt in groups. Once on the move, they feed mainly on shad and other forage fish that don't move as fast in colder temperatures, making them easy prey. Schools of shad will incite a feeding frenzy as the half-starved stripers and sunshines begin to forage after a summer of inactivity.

A favorite hunting tactic of stripers and sunshines is to force schools of baitfish toward the surface or against the shoreline, thus eliminating one avenue of escape. Fishermen seeking stripers and sunshines should look for diving birds feeding on the schooling shad.

Some of the best spots to fish for these bass are Lake Osborne in Palm Beach County, the Apalachicola River in northwest Florida and the St. Johns River in northeast Florida. The most popular places to fish for stripers and sunshines in Lake Osborne are the Sixth Avenue, Lantana and Keller Canal bridges. The best areas in the Apalachicola River are the first 3 or 4 miles below the Jim Woodruff Dam.

Some of the prime striper locations on the St. Johns River system include the power plant outflow on Lake Monroe near Sanford, the jetties at the south end of Lake George in the Astor-Ocala area and along the bombing range craters in Lake George. Other areas include the pilings of all major bridges and the river between lakes Washington and Monroe.

Live shad are the best baits for catching these fish, but lures such as the Shad Rap are effective also. An effective rig for stripers is an egg sinker threaded on the line above a swivel and a hook at the end of a 1½- to 2-foot leader with a live 3- to 4-inch shad. Large shiners will work sometimes.

For sunshine bass, all you need is a lead sinker along with a hook and shrimp fished on bottom. Small shiners and such artificial lures as lead-headed jigs and spoons are effective for sunshines. In deeper water, the deep-running Little George lure sometimes does the trick.

Stripers and sunshines are quite similar in appearance and sometimes even fish biologists have trouble telling them apart. A couple of clues: The stripers have dark horizontal lines running along their bodies. Stripers usually are thinner and longer than sunshines.

Sunshine bass are hybrids obtained by breeding a striped bass and a white bass. They usually can be distinguished by the interrupted zigzag patterns on their sides and a wider, thicker body. However, Vaughn said, he has seen some stripers with broken markings.

The difficulty distinguishing between the two exists only on the St. Johns and Apalachicola because these are the only places the fish are stocked together, Vaughn said.

Stripers have a bag limit of six fish with a minimum length of 15 inches. The sunshine bag limit is 10 a day and no minimum length. According to one fish biologist, difficulties in telling the two apart may prompt a rule change. Both stripers and sunshines are measured from the tip of the mouth to the fork in the tail.

Stripers and sunshines can grow 2 to 3 pounds each year. In Florida, stripers can reach 60 pounds while sunshines may weigh as much as 17 pounds. White bass, in comparison, seldom reach 5 pounds.

State records for striped bass and sunshine bass were caught in Lake Seminole in Jackson County. Justin McAlpin caught a 38-pound, 9-ounce striper on Nov. 15, 1979, and Thomas R. Elder caught a 16-pound, 5-ounce sunshine on May 9, 1985.

Fishing for stripers and sunshines

is good during the cool months. Action usually slows from mid-March when water temperatures start rising until the cooler months of late fall or winter.

Sunshine bass are sterile and striped bass do not reproduce well in Florida. The Florida Game and Fresh Water Fish Commission restocks these species annually. During 1986, the commission stocked 575 miles of rivers and more than 129,500 acres of lakes with more than 2.6 million stripers and sunshines.

Saltwater striped bass were introduced to Florida's fresh water to help control overabundant shad populations. The first hybrid occurred in 1972 by crossing striper females with white bass males. Stripers and sunshine bass can be found throughout the state. The following lakes and streams contain the scrappy stripers and sunshines, which also make for delectable table fare.

Body of water	County	Body of water	County
Wauberg	Alachua	Buffum	Polk
Rowell and Sampson	Bradford	Tsala Apopka	Citrus
Lowry	Clay	Hernando Pool	Citrus
Butler	Union	Inverness Pool	Citrus
Palestine	Union	Apalachicola River	Gadsen
Floral City Pool	Citrus	Star	Polk
Davis	Orange	Gant	Sumter
Thonotosassa	Hillsborough	Ochlockonee River	Liberty
John	Polk	Alto	Alachua
Saddle Creek Park	Polk	Ocean Pond	Baker
Banana	Polk	Hampton	Bradford
Winter Haven Chain of lakes	Polk	Hanna Park	Duval
Lulu	Polk	Cherry	Madison
Shipp	Polk	Francis	Madison
Elouise	Polk	Virginia, Osceola, Mizell	Orange
Rochelle	Polk	Maitland, Minnehaha	Orange
Howard	Polk	Seminole	Pinellas
Smart	Polk	Reedy	Polk
Idylwild	Polk	Pine	Palm Beach
Fanny	Polk	Catherine	Palm Beach
Haines	Polk	Clarke	Palm Beach
Hartridge	Polk	St. Johns River	Putnam
Osborne	Palm Beach	Talquin	Leon
Watertown	Columbia	Blue Cypress	Indian River
Harris	Lake	Seminole	Jackson
Griffin	Lake	Harney	Volusia
Carlton	Lake	Monroe	Volusia, Seminole
Apopka	Orange	Jessup	Seminole
Escambia River	Santa Rosa	Parker	Polk
Yellow River	Santa Rosa	Moody	Polk
Choctawhatchee River	Washington	Manatee Reservoir	Manatee
Munson	Leon	Santa Fe	Bradford
Ella	Leon	Kingsby	Clay
Newnans	Alachua	Crosby	Bradford

Trolling is an excellent way to catch stripers and sunshines because the fish spend much of their time in open water chasing shad. Use shad or minnow-type lures, spoons, jigs and spinnerfly lures. And don't overlook live bait. Fish on or near the bottom with shiners or minnows — and sometimes even cut bait. Using minnows at night is effective. Use a bright light to attract fish. The Howey Bridge on the Clermont Chain in Lake County is a good night spot for sunshine bass.

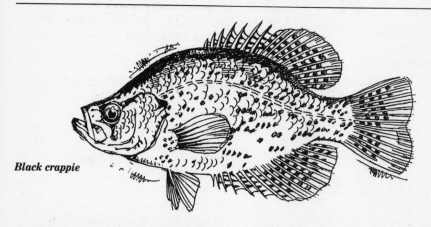

Black crappie

Speckled perch (Crappie): Specks, as Floridians call them, are a favorite cold-weather gamefish. They also have a reputation as the best-tasting freshwater fish in Florida's lakes and streams.

For a relaxing outing, grab a cane pole and a bucket of Missouri minnows and spend the day drifting in search of a stringer full of crappie. But there may not be time to relax if you catch them when they're spawning. Then you may need two poles.

This is a good time to use a small jig such as the Bream Killer or Speck Killer and an ultralight rod and reel for best jigging action. Cast the jig, let it sink and then retrieve it slowly. Beetle Spins and other minijigs are good lures to use when you run into a speck congregation.

Speckled perch are caught almost exclusively during the spawning season. They begin congregating during the first cold weather and remain concentrated for spawning until the early spring. The most popular method for taking crappie is to drift with Missouri minnows or small shiners floating from a small, cone-shaped cork. Experienced anglers get results with jigs and spinnerbaits.

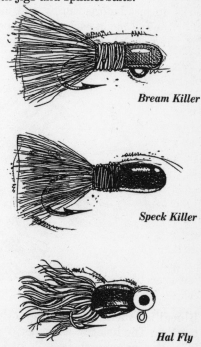

Bream Killer

Speck Killer

Hal Fly

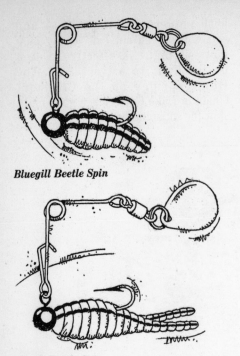

Bluegill Beetle Spin

Speck Beetle Spin

shoreline vegetation; grass, lily pads and brush are favorite places. Use a speck hook (No. 2 size is good), a small split shot and a cork. Search for specks in several inches to several feet of water. Keep dropping your minnow along the cattails, grass or lily pads until you find them. Try not to disturb the fish when you anchor. Get ready for some fast action. Specks weighing as much as 4 pounds have been caught in Florida waters.

When the water starts cooling off in late fall, fishermen can usually find specks by drifting in open water with several poles dangling over the side of the boat and with Missouri minnows drifting just off the bottom. For best results, hook the minnows through both lips.

The limit for panfish is 50 a day, including speckled perch, bluegills, shellcrackers or any other fish bearing a resemblance to the sunfish family. Take home enough for supper and let the rest go. For a true Cracker meal, roll specks in meal and deep-fry them along with corndodgers (hushpuppies). Boil a pot of yellow grits to go with them.

Crappie usually start spawning by early January and continue through March or early April. Action usually picks up just before, during and just after the full moon each month. Look for them in shallow water around

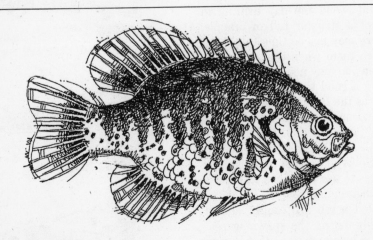

Bluegill

Bluegills, shellcrackers and other panfish: The bluegill, a smaller cousin of the largemouth bass, is one of the most abundant and sought-after

fish in Florida. It also is the sweetest tasting. You can find them in almost any body of water in the state. This scrappy fighter gets its name from the dark blue coloration around its gill cover and ear flaps. They are often referred to as copperheads because of the copper coloring on many of the males.

The adult bluegill is about two-thirds as wide as it is long and can use its shape to its advantage when hooked. Pound for pound, the bluegill is perhaps the best of all fighters that frequent Florida's fresh waters.

From late spring to early fall, male bluegills go to the shallow water where they congregate with other males to sweep shallow beds around the sandy areas. These beds usually are in a cluster and may be seen in clear water as a honeycomb of white spots on the lake bottom. Each pair of bluegills may produce as many as 40,000 young.

Bluegills will hit throughout the year, but tend to hit best during the spawning months, especially around full-moon time each month. During the winter months, bluegills usually go to deeper water and are harder to locate.

Redear sunfish

Another panfish favorite is the shellcracker or "redear," which is closely related to the bluegill. They often are confused with the bluegill because of similar size and coloration. A red, crescent-shaped spot on the back side of the ear flap (thus redear) is one way of telling the two bream apart. The name "shellcracker" comes from the hard palate used to crush small snails and mussels. Bottom-fishing with live redworms along mussel beds is a good way to locate redears. East Lake Tohopekaliga in Central Florida has a large mussel bed area near the middle of the lake that yields some large catches.

Redears spawn very much like bluegills, but they usually spawn earlier in the spring. This is the best time to catch them. While bluegills will hit earthworms, crickets, spinner-baits, popping bugs or jigs, the shell-crackers prefer live worms. Use a cane pole, light monofilament line (2- to 6-pound test), a small split shot, and a No. 4 or No. 6 hook. Hook a couple of redworms so they can wiggle and drop the bait on the bottom. Then, hang on for a good fight.

Other panfish that offer excellent fishing and taste include the stump-nocker, a spotted sunfish, and the redbreast sunfish. The stumpnocker usually is caught in rivers and streams. It gets its name from its habitat — cypress trees and tree roots. They can be caught on warm spring days by accurately casting small spinnerbaits against the bank and slowly retrieving the bait to deeper water.

Redbreast sunfish

The redbreast sunfish also frequents rivers and streams. It is readily indentified by the bright red spot on its breast. Males have a more distinct patch than the females. The best time to catch the redbreast is during the spring with crickets, earthworms, spinnerbaits or artificial popping bugs.

Another Florida game fish with a bag limit is the pickerel. Although the red-finned pickerel is grouped in the 50-panfish-a-day limit, the chain pickerel is in a category all its own. The chain pickerel, a cousin of the northern pike, has a bag limit of 15 a day. Called a chain pickerel because of the chainlike markings on its body, the fish is long and bony, but it can be eaten if filleted and cut in a crisscross fashion with a razor blade and fried to a crispy texture. The pickerel will go for an occasional shiner or flashy spoon. They especially like to frequent weedy areas of lakes.

Although it is not a game fish, the catfish is an exceptional fighter when hooked. One of my greatest battles was with a 7½-pound channel cat caught on a small bream hook, leader and flyrod. I was wading at the time and it took me 15 minutes to land it.

Florida's catfish are primarily channel cats, white cats, brown bull-

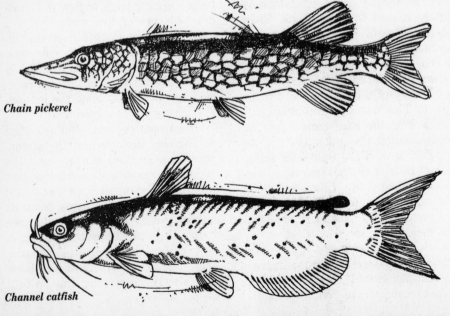

Chain pickerel

Channel catfish

heads and spotted catfish. They will hit live bait, shiners, Missouri minnows, redworms, certain lures and cut shad or blood bait. They also go for chicken necks and liver. Some trot-liners have caught them on soap and watermelon rind. Catfish are very tasty, especially the smaller Okeechobee and river cats.

The American shad, a saltwater shad that returns to the St. Johns and other sites to spawn, offers sportsmen seasonal action when they begin their yearly migration. Small jigs such as the Shad Dart are trolled slowly behind the boat along the rivers where shad are known to frequent. They have tender mouths and must be fought without putting too much pressure on the fish. Some Floridians consider them good eating although they are a bit on the bony side.

Other fish that offer great sport but little taste include the garfish and mudfish. Any fisherman who has ever wasted a dozen shiners on a school of garfish can attest to their being elusive. Once hooked, however, they put up a good fight.

The mudfish, a prehistoric creature with some sharp, mean jaws, has fooled many a bass fisherman into thinking he had a record largemouth on the line. Mudfish are strong fighters and can live for hours out of water. When lakes and creeks go dry, the mudfish will bury itself in the mud and wait for the water to rise, thus its name. It is called other things, some of which cannot be printed. It will hit live shiners and plastic worms without hesitation.

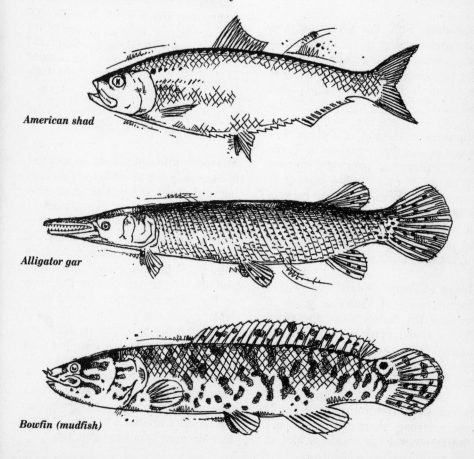

American shad

Alligator gar

Bowfin (mudfish)

FISHING TERMS

Chumming: Laying mash, chicken pellets or other feed thrown into the water to attract fish. Use redworms for bait. Chumming is especially good for attracting freshwater mullet. To catch native shiners to use as fish bait, toss bread in the water. Then use a small hook baited with a dough ball or small piece of worm to catch your own bait.

Crankbait: Bait that is cast out and runs under water, requiring no extra action from the fisherman. A crankbait is retrieved simply by reeling it in. Speed of the retrieval can be varied.

Flipping: A method of fishing that uses a plastic flipping worm or Texas rig. The fisherman gets right up next to the weeds and flips — instead of casts — the worm or eel into pockets in the weeds. Let the lure drop and sit for a few seconds before repeating the procedure as you continue working pockets in the weeds.

Grass shrimp: Small freshwater shrimp found in shoreline grass in many of the state's lakes and river. These small crustaceans can be dipped from the grass with small mesh nets. They are excellent natural bait for almost any freshwater fish.

Jigger pole fishing: Use a heavy pole, a strong, short line and a pork rind or other large weedless lure to fish in the weeds for big bass. The fisherman makes lots of noise with the pole to make the fish angry enough to hit. This sort of fishing is usually done at night.

Jigging: Use a jig and fish around weeds and structures. Deep jigging is used to fish deep-water holes during extremely cold or hot months. Deep jigging requires a lot of patience because the jig or spoon must be worked slowly along the bottom.

Lunker: Large bass that tips the scales at 7 pounds or more. Definitions vary with the fisherman. Some call a 5-pound bass a lunker.

Missouri minnow: A small minnow used mostly for speckled perch fishing. Originally shipped in from Missouri, they also come from Arkansas and other states. Other fish including catfish, sunshine bass and warmouths will hit a Missouri minnow. Native shiners, on the other hand, are larger and are used to catch larger fish such as the largemouth and striped bass. Native shiners are found in local lakes, and the best way to use them is to catch them in the lake you plan to fish and fish with them right then. Imported shiners brought in from Arkansas and other states have a longer life span in captivity. Battery-operated aerators are used to keep shiners and Missouri minnows alive.

Panfish: Speckled perch, bluegills, shellcrackers (redears), redbreast and other types of smaller sunfish.

Spinnerbaits: Baits with shiny blades on them to attract fish. Smaller spinnerbaits such as Beetle Spins are used to catch panfish. Larger spinnerbaits such as weedless spinners with a bucktail or pork rind are effective lures for largemouth bass — especially in brushy areas.

Texas rig: A combination of a bullet lead and a 2/0 to 5/0 hook, which is barely run through the head of the worm and then back into the worm to make it weedless.

Trolling: Moving slowly with the lure well behind the boat. When the fish are feeding near the surface, use shallow-running lures. When they're near the bottom, use deep-running lures. Vary your trolling speed until you find the speed that's right for you.

KINDS OF HOOKS

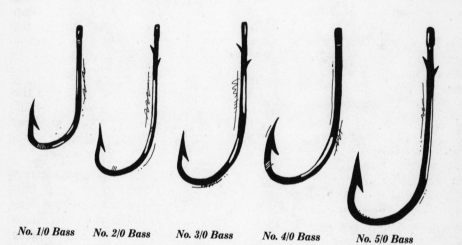

No. 1/0 Bass *No. 2/0 Bass* *No. 3/0 Bass* *No. 4/0 Bass* *No. 5/0 Bass*

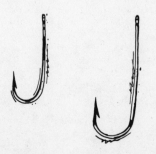

No. 6 Panfish *No. 2 Panfish*

2

RECORD CATCHES

Every bass angler fantasizes about topping the world record for largemouth bass set in 1932 — 22 pounds, 4 ounces. If the world record seems out of sight, there's the state record to aim for. The Florida record largemouth — 20 pounds, 2 ounces — was caught in 1923. Catching a world record bass today would be worth more than a million dollars in endorsements and appearances.

The Florida Game and Fresh Water Fish Commission has still another category, Big Catch, given for catches that meet minimum qualifying weights. To be certified, however, the fish must be verified by an authorized commission biologist or other qualified employee and must be weighed on a certified scale. If you catch a lunker that meets these requirements, contact the nearest commission office. If you do not have a local Florida Game and Fresh Water Fish Commission in your town, contact the regional office.

Northwest, Panama City,
(904) 265-3676 or (800) 342-1676

Northeast, Lake City, (904) 752-0353
or (800) 342-8105

Central, Ocala, (904) 629-8162
or (800) 342-9620

South, Lakeland (813) 644-9269
or (800) 282-8002

Everglades, West Palm Beach
(305) 683-0748 or (800) 432-2046

FLORIDA RECORDS
As of May 11, 1987.

Largemouth bass: 20 pounds, 2 ounces. Caught May 1923 by Frederick Joseph Friebel on Big Fish Lake, a private pond in Pasco County.

Striped bass: 38 pounds, 9 ounces. 41¼ inches total length, 28¾ inches girth. Caught Nov. 15, 1979, by Justin McAlpin on Lake Seminole in Gadsden County.

Sunshine bass: 16 pounds, 5 ounces. 32 inches total length, 22 inches girth. Caught May 9, 1985, by Thomas R. Elder on Lake Seminole in Jackson County.

White bass: 4 pounds, 11 ounces. 18¾ inches total length, 18¼ inches girth. Caught April 9, 1982, by Richard Steven Davis on the Apalachicola River below the Jim Woodruff Dam, Gadsen County.

Suwannee bass: 3 pounds, 14¼ ounces. Caught March 2, 1985, by Ronnie Everett on the Suwannee River in Gilchrist County.

Redeye bass: 7 pounds. 22½ inches total length. Caught June 16, 1982, by J.T. Reynolds on the Apalachicola River in Gadsden County.

Spotted bass: 3 pounds, 12 ounces. 18¼ inches total length. Caught June 24, 1985, by Dow Gilmore on the Apalachicola River in Gulf County.

Crappie (speckled perch): 3 pounds, 12 ounces. 18 inches total length. Caught Dec. 29, 1964, by John McGilvary on Newnans Lake in Alachua County.

Joey Floyd

Shellcracker (redear): 4 pounds, 13¾ ounces. 17½ inches total length, 16½ inches girth. Caught March 13, 1986, by Joey Floyd on Merritt's Mill Pond in Jackson County.

Bluegill: 2 pounds, 14 ounces. 12⅜ inches total length, 16¼ inches girth. Caught March 31, 1985, by Seth Branch on a private pond in Columbia County.

Redbreast: 1 pound, 12.8 ounces. 12⅛ inches total length. Caught May 29, 1984, on the Suwannee River in Dixie County.

Redfin pickerel: 10½ ounces. 13½ inches total length. Caught April 20, 1985, by Carlton Ingram on a small pond in Leon County.

Channel catfish: 44 pounds, 8 ounces. 43 inches total length. Caught May 19, 1985, by Joe Purvis on Lake Bluff in Lake County.

White catfish: 16 pounds, 12 ounces. 32 inches total length. Caught April 24, 1984, by Shawn J. Williams on the Caloosahatchee River in Lee County.

Carp: 40 pounds, 9 ounces. 45 inches total length. Caught May 24, 1981, by Bernard Rowan on the Apalachicola River in Gadsden County.

Long-nosed gar: 41 pounds. 58½ inches total length. Caught April 14, 1985, by Evan Merritt on Lake Panasoffkee in Sumter County.

Mudfish (bowfin): 19 pounds. 32½ inches total length. Caught Nov. 5, 1984, by Jim Brown on Lake Kissimmee in Osceola County.

American shad: 4 pounds, 10 ounces. 20.9 inches total length. Caught Feb. 23, 1985, by Phil Chapman on the St. Johns River in Seminole County.

FLORIDA FRESHWATER FISH QUALIFYING WEIGHTS

Under the Game and Fresh Water Fish Commission's certification standards, a largemouth bass must meet the minimum qualifying weight of 14 pounds. While a 14-pounder won't break any records, it does earn the fisherman state recognition. Billy M. O'Berry caught a 17-pound, 4½-ounce lunker in Polk County in 1986.

The minimum qualifying weights for other Florida freshwater fish are:

Redeye bass	5 pounds
Spotted bass	2½ pounds
Suwannee bass	3 pounds
Striped bass	25 pounds
White bass	3½ pounds
Sunshine bass	14 pounds
Black crappie (speck)	3 pounds
Bluegill	2 pounds
Redbreasted sunfish	1½ pounds
Redear sunfish (shellcracker)	3 pounds
Spotted sunfish	10 ounces
Warmouth sunfish	1¼ pounds
Chain pickerel	6 pounds
Redfin pickerel	10 ounces
Carp	30 pounds
Channel catfish	30 pounds
White catfish	14 pounds
Mudfish (bowfin)	15 pounds
Long-nose gar	25 pounds
American shad	3 pounds

No state records have been established for the alligator gar and the Florida gar, but according to the fish commission, the minimum weights for qualifying are 70 pounds for the alligator gar and 5 pounds for the Florida gar.

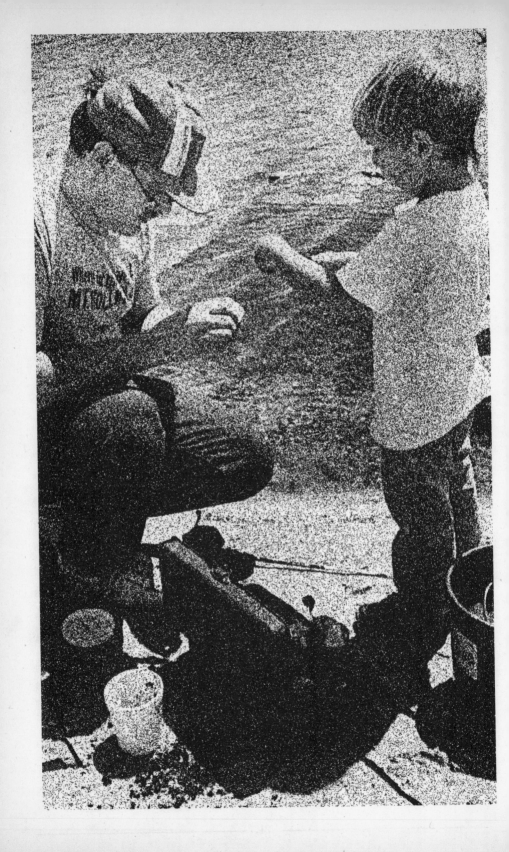

3

HANDLE WITH CARE

My dad taught me not to keep any fish unless I planned to eat them. That was hard to understand as a youngster, but as I get older I find myself leaning more toward that philosophy.

Today, more anglers are releasing the fish they catch. Bass tournament fishermen stress the program, and often the angler is penalized if he reports to the weigh-in with dead fish. I release most of the bass I catch. Occasionally I will keep a few for dinner if we're having company or if I am especially hungry for some fresh bass fillets. The same is true for bluegills and shellcrackers. I probably release 95 percent of all the fish I catch — except speckled perch and spotted sea trout. I am fond of both.

Some fishing tournaments impose a minimum size limit although there is no state-imposed limit. If you plan to release the fish, you must be careful handling them or they will die later.

Damage to fish usually results from careless or improper handling.

If you plan to keep your catch, there are some rules to follow to keep it from winding up in the garbage can. Of course, the best way to keep fish fresh from the lake or river to the frying pan is to cook them on the spot. There's nothing like pulling up to an island or the riverbank and frying up a mess of fish and hushpuppies. However, the fish seem to develop lockjaw whenever I take a skillet, some meal and fat along on a trip. Some guides will cook your catch for lunch. They call it a shore dinner.

Live wells will help keep your fish alive until you return to shore. Deterioration begins as soon as the fish dies. The speed of the flavor-tainting process is influenced by water temperature — the warmer the water or environment, the faster the decline.

In many commercial fisheries, the catch is often iced down for cleaning later. Others clean first, then cool, freeze or can the fish, according to Mercury Marine's outdoor research department. Sports anglers can use similar techniques with the added benefit of keeping the fish alive. Live wells with aerators help keep the fish alive even in hot weather and high water temperatures.

Using a net often reduces the amount of physical contact with the fish. It also is the surest way to get a fish under control without wrestling it into the boat. By using the net, you don't have to handle the fish as much, which often results in removal of the protective mucus from the fish. When the mucus is removed, the fish is more susceptible to disease.

If you prefer to grasp the fish, avoid squeezing it and thus damaging its internal organs. When grasping a bass, you can render it immobile by clamping the lower jaw between thumb and forefinger. But don't try this method on a toothy chain pickerel. The pickerel and other fish with sharp teeth can be handled by getting a grip over the head and gill covers — not behind them. Small fish hooked on a fly can often be shaken free by the angler holding the hook. Release the small fish so they can grow up to give you a good battle later.

When plastic worms or barbs from hooks are swallowed by bass, it is better to cut the line. Don't try to remove the hook; you will only damage the fish and probably cause it to die. Some hook remover devices can help reach the hard-to-get-to spots, but metal in a fish disintegrates rapidly. Let nature take its course.

Always release bass during spawning season. The females are often laden with roe and the males are needed to guard the small fry until they are large enough to fend for themselves.

Another effective method of keeping your catch alive is a wire basket hung over the side of the boat. Fish stringers are good for the short-term, but don't forget to pull the stringer aboard when moving the boat. John Pitts, a fishing pal, and I fished along the Kissimmee Chain all day for a mess of specks for dinner only to have them stripped off when we forgot to pull the stringer in before our trip to the dock. That can be a real letdown for the fisherman and hard to explain to his wife after he's been on the river all day and returns home with an empty stringer. Cottonmouths and alligators do their part to empty stringers also.

The secret to fresh fish: Clean them quickly and cool or freeze them. I usually freeze a couple of half-gallon milk jugs before a fishing trip. They keep the fish cold and provide drinking water. To freeze fish, I put them in quart or half-gallon milk cartons and fill the cartons with water. Sometimes I use freezer bags instead and fill them with water before freezing. If you don't want to store the fish in water, squeeze lemon juice over them before freezing.

If you fillet your catch first it will take up less space in the freezer. I do that with most of the fish I catch — with the exception of bluegills, specks and an occasional bass for broiling. Bluegills and smaller specks I like to fry whole and very crispy.

Use a sharp knife to clean fish. It makes the task much easier and makes for less waste. My 10-inch Rapala fillet knife works well. Also use a whetstone to sharpen your knife, or, if you prefer, a Butterfly type sharpener, which does a quick easy job. To fillet a fish I use the method recommended by Rapala (see page 26).

If you decide not to fillet your fish and want to preserve it whole, scale the fish before gutting it. You may want to use a fish-cleaning board that has a clamp to hold the fish. You can find these rather inexpensive boards at most tackle shops. Sometimes I use a teaspoon to clean speckled perch, bluegills or shellcrackers. Other times, I use a fish scaler. There are several types and these, too, can be found in tackle shops. When scaling a fish, move the scaler upward from the tail to the head.

The next step is to remove the head. Place the blade of a sharp fillet knife just behind the head and make a semicircular cut downward.

When cleaning bluegills, I usually make a cut halfway down from behind the head and then pull it off with my hand. This way, most of the innards are removed along with the head. If this method doesn't appeal to you, take the point of your knife blade and make a slice from the belly to the section near the tail and remove the insides. After hosing out the stomach cavity until it is clean,

you may or may not want to remove the fins. I like to fry panfish until they are very crisp and then eat the crunchy tails and some of the fins. If this isn't your kettle of fish, remove the fins with your knife.

Fish skinners work best for cleaning catfish. They are similar to pliers, but are much better at gripping and skinning a fish. Grasp the catfish behind the two lateral fins with one hand and make a downward slice — just through the skin — on each side of the fish just behind the gills. Using the skinners, peel the skin back toward the tail. Cut around each fin to loosen it and grasp the fins with the skinners to remove them. Finally, gut the catfish and cut off its head.

A reminder: Do not clean your fish in the same water you kept them in after catching them. It could be polluted. Unless facilities are provided at the site, wait until you get home to clean them.

HOW TO FILLET
A FISH

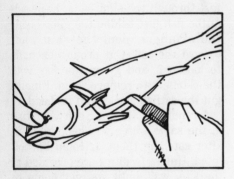

1 Make the first cut just behind the gills and slice down to the bone. Without removing the blade, turn it and slice straight along the backbone to the tail.

2 After slicing the fillet off at the tail, turn the fish over and repeat the first step on the other side.

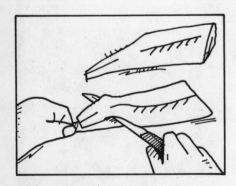

5 To remove the skin, insert the knife at the tail and cut the meat from the skin.

6 Now fillets are ready for the pan or freezer. Remember not to overwash fillets to preserve the tasty juices and to keep meat in its firm natural state.

Fillet instructions courtesy of Normark Corp. (sole distributors of Rapala products).

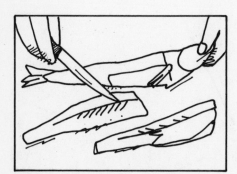

3 Removing both sides enables you to cut both fillets without disturbing the entrails for a fast and neat way to prepare fish.

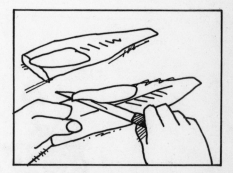

4 To finish the fillets, remove the rib section. To avoid wasting meat, use a sharp, flexible knife. Insert the blade close to the rib bones and slice away the entire section. Do this before removing the skin to keep waste to a minimum.

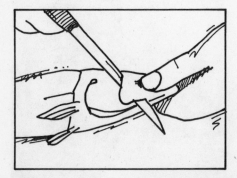

7 You may want to cut out the cheeks, which some fishermen know is the filet mignon of the fish. Though small, they're tasty and worth saving.

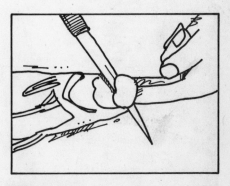

8 Slice into the cheek where indicated. Scoop out the meat with the blade, peeling away the skin. Repeat on the other side.

4

FISH FIXIN'S

I recall a fishing trip when my dad and I pulled up to an island to deep-fry a mess of bass and speckled perch. As he cooked, my dad put the fish in one stack and the hushpuppies in another on our old folding camp table. As the sweet aroma filled the air, an inebriated fisherman followed his nose to our campsite.

"That fish has a delicious aroma," the tipsy angler said.

"Why don't you help yourself to some," my dad replied.

"Sure you have enough?"

"We have plenty," my dad insisted.

The fisherman, apparently famished, sat down against a large tree trunk and helped himself to the hushpuppies. I thought it strange that he never once sampled the fish, but chose instead to fill up on hushpuppies.

"That's the best damn fish I ever ate," he said, shaking my dad's hand. "There wasn't a bone in it."

It spoke well of my dad's hushpuppies.

One of my favorite ways of cooking fish is to deep-fry them in peanut oil. In my years of cooking fish, I've learned a few shortcuts. I use Alabama Ground Corn Meal and mix in some salt. It's fluffy and gets the fish good and crisp. For hushpuppies, I use the Dixie Lily mix in the red bag. It already has an onion taste. All you have to do is add water and wait 10 minutes.

The Gulf and South Atlantic Fisheries Development Foundation recommends these cooking methods:

WAYS TO PREPARE YOUR CATCH

Baking: To cook by dry heat, place fish in a greased baking dish. Keep the fish moist and flavorful with seasoned oil, sauce or any condiment of your choice while baking. Fillets and steaks can easily be adapted to many recipes that require baking. A dressed fish may be stuffed with an herb and bread stuffing and baked with the head and tail still attached. Bake in a moderate 350 F oven until fish flakes easily when tested with a fork. Cooking time varies according to thickness.

Broiling: To cook by direct, intense heat, choose pan-dressed fish, fillets or steaks. Place fish in a single layer on a well-greased broiler pan. Baste well with oil or basting sauce before and during cooking. The fish should be about 4 to 6 inches from the heat source. Cooking time is about 10 minutes. Turn thicker pieces halfway through and baste.

Charcoal broiling: Select pan-dressed fish, fillets or steaks and cook over hot briquettes in charcoal, electric or gas grill. Thick cuts are better. A well-greased, long-handled hinged wire grill is recommended for ease in turning. Baste fish with sauce before and during broiling. Broil about 4 to 6 inches from moderately hot briquettes for 10 to 20 minutes, depending on thickness. Fish is done when it flakes easily.

Boiling: Bring water to a boil in a big pot. Use 2 tablespoons of salt for each quart of water. Add fish or crabs and return to a boil before reducing heat to maintain a slow boil. Fish need about 8 to 10 minutes; crabs, 12 to 15. Fish usually are boiled when they are to be served with a sauce or flaked and combined with other ingredients.

Poaching: Place fish in a single layer in a wide, shallow pan or frying pan. Barely cover with liquid — lightly salted water, water seasoned with herbs and spices, milk or a mixture of white wine and water. Simmer for 5 to 8 minutes or until fish flakes easily when tested with a fork. Poached fish can be served as an entree with a sauce, as a main ingredient in a casserole or chilled and flaked for a salad or dip.

Steaming: Use a deep pan with a tight cover if a steam cooker is not available. Use anything for a steaming rack that will keep the fish out of the water while it boils. The water can be plain or seasoned with spices. Bring the water to a rapid boil and place fish on the rack. Cover the pan tightly and steam for about 8 to 10 minutes. Serve the same as poached.

Deep-fat frying: Cook fish in a deep layer of oil or fat — but not more than half full. Place breaded or batter-dipped fish, one layer at a time, in a fry basket so the pieces don't touch. Fry at 350 F to 375 F until fish is brown and flakes easily with a fork.

Bring oil to the correct temperature before adding fish. If you don't have a fry basket, simply drop the fish into the hot oil: it will float to the top and turn brown when it is done. A pair of long tongs is handy for removing the fish.

Pan frying: Use a small amount of hot oil — about an eighth of an inch in the bottom of a thick frying pan. Place breaded fish in a single layer in the hot oil. Do not overload. Fry fish at a moderate temperature until it is lightly browned on one side, then turn and cook on the other side until browned.

Oven frying: Dip fish in salted milk and coat with a breading mixture of your choice. Next, place fish in a shallow, well-greased baking pan. Pour melted fat or oil over the fish and bake it in a 500 F oven until it flakes easily. When cooking this way, you do not have to turn or baste. Cooking time is short, so this one's a good method to use when serving large groups.

Smoking: Place fish in a covered charcoal grill — electric or gas will also work — skin side down and baste frequently. Add water-soaked wood chips to the briquettes to produce the smoke and then lower the temperature. I put the charcoal briquettes on one side of the grill, soak hickory chips in water and add them to the charcoal from time to time. I put the fish on the other side of the grill, away from the charcoal. Then I smoke the fish for several hours, adding wet chips at least every 45 minutes or so.

Planking: Bake dressed fish, steaks or fillets on a plank made especially for this purpose. Using liquid shortening, carefully oil a hardwood plank or board and heat slowly in the oven. Brush with oil and bake in a 350 F oven until the fish flakes easily. Remove the fish from the oven and arrange hot mashed potatoes and vegetables around the fish and serve on the plank.

Microwave cooking: It's best to follow the manufacturer's directions for best results using this method because oven settings vary with brands. Generally speaking, fish is cooked at high temperatures to retain natural goodness, texture and flavor.

Some special recipes

Smoked
FISH PATE

3 cups of flaked, smoked fish (remove skin and bones before flaking)
2 packages (8 oz. ea.) cream cheese, softened
3 tablespoons lemon juice
2 tablespoons grated onion
3 tablespoons chopped parsley

Assorted crackers
Combine cheese, lemon juice and grated onion. Whip until smooth and fluffy. Stir in fish and chopped parsley. Chill for one hour. Garnish with parsley and serve with crackers. Makes 3½ cups.

Fish STEW

1½ lbs. fillets
1 teaspoon salt
½ cup boiling water
1 chicken bouillon cube
1½ lbs. frozen stewed vegetables
1 can (10¾ oz.) cream of chicken soup
½ cup light cream
½ teaspoon white pepper
2 tablespoons dry white wine
Chopped parsley for garnish
Sprinkle fish with salt and cut large, skinned fillets in half. Roll fillets into turbans and secure with a wooden pick. Pour boiling water into a 4-quart soup pot and

dissolve bouillon cube. Add stew vegetables. Cover and cook over low heat for 10 to 15 minutes or until vegetables are tender. Combine soup, light cream and pepper. Pour soup mixture over vegetables and mix well. Bring mixture to a boil and add fish rolls. Reduce heat, cover and cook over low heat for 10 to 12 minutes or until fish flakes easily when tested with a fork. Remove wooden picks and stir in wine. Garnish with chopped parsley. Makes 6 servings.

Tartar Sauce

1 cup mayonnaise or salad dressing
2 tablespoons chopped parsley
2 tablespoons finely chopped sweet pickle
2 tablespoons finely chopped green olives (with pimentos)
2 tablespoons finely chopped onion
1 teaspoon cream style horseradish
1 teaspoon lemon juice
⅛ teaspoon Worcestershire sauce
⅛ teaspoon salt
⅛ teaspoon liquid hot pepper sauce

Combine all ingredients and mix well. Makes 1½ cups.

Fish Casserole

2 cups cooked flaked fish
1 cup chopped celery
¼ cup margarine or butter, melted
1 can (10¾ oz.) condensed cream mushroom soup
1 cup cracker crumbs
3 hard-cooked eggs, chopped
¼ cup shredded cheddar cheese
½ cup shredded cheddar cheese
Paprika

Cook celery in butter in 10-inch skillet until tender. Add fish, soup, cracker crumbs, eggs and ¼ cup cheese and mix well. Place fish mixture in a well-greased 1½ quart casserole dish. Sprinkle with the ½ cup of cheese and paprika. Bake in a 375 F oven for 25 minutes or until thoroughly heated and the cheese is melted. Makes 6 servings.

LEMON BUTTER SAUCE

½ cup margarine or butter, melted
2 tablespoons lemon juice
Combine butter and lemon juice and heat. Makes ½ cup of sauce that goes well with any broiled fish.

FISH A LA PEPPER

1½ pounds of fish fillets
½ teaspoon instant chicken broth
1 teaspoon garlic salt
½ teaspoon lemon pepper
½ cup boiling water
2 tablespoons vegetable oil
¼ cup tomato sauce
1 teaspoon capers
½ medium green pepper cut into rings
½ medium red pepper cut into rings

Cut fish into 4-inch pieces. Dissolve instant chicken broth in water. Sprinkle fish with garlic salt and lemon pepper. Cook fish in oil in a 12-inch non-stick fry pan over moderate heat for 5 minutes, turning often. Add broth, tomato sauce and capers to fish. Reduce heat; cover and simmer for 10 minutes. Top with pepper rings and cook 5 minutes longer or until fish flakes easily with a fork and peppers are tender. Makes 4 servings.

BASS FILLETS
A LA ONIONS AND MAYONNAISE

This recipe comes from my son, Bob, and is a simple but great-tasting way to prepare bass.

Take several bass fillets and place on aluminum foil. Cover with a thick layer of mayonnaise. Slice an onion and place rings on top of mayonnaise. Add salt and pepper to taste. Fold foil to cover fillets. Punch a few holes in foil to let smoke in. Place foil on hot grill. Place wet hickory chips on charcoal briquettes. Close the grill lid and cook for 15 to 20 minutes.

SMOKED MULLET
SPREAD

This comes from my wife, Donna, and is one of our favorites.

1 cup flaked smoked mullet
  ½ cup finely diced onions
  ½ teaspoon horseradish
  1 teaspoon worcestershire sauce
  a few dashes of hot sauce or
tabasco
  ½ teaspoon dill weed
  2 tablespoons spicy mustard
  ½ teaspoon lemon juice

1 cup of mayonnaise
salt and pepper to taste
Mix all these ingredients well, chill and serve with crackers.

———

Except for the last two, all recipes come from *Seafood Adventures*, the Gulf and South Atlantic Fisheries Development Foundation's recipe book.

5

FISHING TIPS

Keep your eyes and ears open around veteran fishermen. You just might get a line on a secret or some new technique. For instance, I always managed to catch a few bass when using a plastic worm-Texas rig combination in one Central Florida lake. One day I saw an angler boat a 10-pound largemouth on a crankbait. I got a good look at the lure he was using as he eased by me. It was a plug that resembled a shad, a baitfish plentiful in that lake. I got myself to the nearest tackle shop and looked over all the lures until I found that one.

A technique I picked up from another angler — after years of trial and error — was an effective way of catching bass on plastic worm rigs. I let them run too long before setting the hook. In his book *Catch Bass*, noted bass authority Doug Hannon suggests setting the hook almost immediately after the bass takes the plastic worm. Hannon recommends using a sharp 2/0 hook instead of a larger hook. When he feels the telltale tap, Hannon drops his rod tip and brings it overhead almost immediately to set the hook. I count to three. It works.

Another book that may give you some ideas is Larry Larsen's *Productive Tactics for Shallow Water Bass.* Fishing magazines that may point you to some new techniques and good fishing holes include *Florida Sportsman, Outdoor Life, Sports Afield,* and *Field & Stream.*

Tackle shop owners and fishing marina operators are helpful when it comes to finding out where the fish are biting and what they're biting. When fishing a new area, it's not a bad idea to hire a fishing guide the first day.

MORE ANGLES

Stomach analysis: A stomach analysis can reveal what foods the fish are feeding on, and thus, what to use and where to go for the best results. If crayfish or aquatic insects are found, use diving lures or bait on the bottom. The second largest bass on record was caught on a crawdad on a lake bottom. When minnows show up, use either natural bait or jigs around submerged brush or similar haunts. Grasshoppers, beetles, or other land creatures are a signal to cast against the bank using shallow-running lures or surface plugs.

Fishing river snags: Downed trees, stumps, brush and other debris found in rivers and streams play an important role by providing cover for fish, turtles, insects, snails and mussels. Where there are snags, there are more and larger fish, according to biologists, who found that in one snagless stream fish weighed 25 percent less. So the next time you hook into a snag, instead of cursing your luck, be glad: You've located a fish habitat.

Float fishing the rivers: Float fishermen have to be innovative. Unlike lake anglers, the river angler is seldom in a spot long enough to determine a pattern and lure that are best for that spot. Че must experiment until he finds a winning combination. One successful lure used by float fishermen in search of bass and panfish is the spinner. While the usual weighted spinning lures work fine, angling experts at Mercury outboards have found that a bucktail fly and spinner combo, similar to that used by flycasters, is a deadly lure for stream fishing.

The bucktail-spinner can be adapted to spinner and spin-casting tackle. The trick is to make sure the lure is heavy enough to cast accurately, and to descend in water deep enough to tempt the fish from beneath logs and rocks. The current and speed of your boat floating downstream play a part in how quickly the lure reaches the fish.

Again, borrowing from the fly fish-

erman, you can add a strip of lead wire to the shaft of the spinner to increase the weight of the lure. Be careful to wind it on so it will not impede the revolving blade. If lead wire isn't handy, a small split shot can be substituted, although it must be pinched on the line ahead of the spinner. A large, full-bodied bucktail fly is attached behind the spinner. Brown, black or gray with a touch of red showing are excellent colors. Size depends on whether you're after bass or panfish.

Mounting a lunker: Don't clean a trophy lunker before taking it to the taxidermist to have it mounted. Cleaning it will ruin it. Wrap it carefully in a wet cloth and freeze it whole. The taxidermist will correct any color loss.

Water temperature: Most fish prefer a definite water temperature at any given time. When you catch your first fish of the day, try to determine the temperature of the water from which it came. Use a temperature meter and line measure to show depth in feet. It's likely that you will find more of the same at that depth.

Tying monofilament lines: Monofilament fishing lines are easier to tie and make stronger knots when wet. To get the strongest knots, simply dip your line in the water before tying a lure to the line. The knot will slip easier and the line will not weaken as much at the tie point.

IMPROVED CLINCH KNOT

This knot ranks as one of the most widely used today.
It is easy to tie and strong.

1. Run end of line through eye of hook or lure.

2. Loop around standing part of line 5 or 6 times.

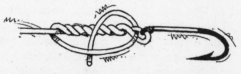

3. Thread tag end back between the eye and the coils as shown and then back through the hoop.

4. Pull up tight and trim tag end.

Stripping line from reels: Tired of yanking and pulling old line from your reels? Berkley and Company makes a hand-held battery-powered line stripper that strips line from fishing reels in seconds. The line stripper sells for about $10 in most tackle stores. It has a built-in hook sharpener also.

How to fill your spool: When filling a spool on your fishing reel, have someone hold a pencil through the center of the spool so it will turn freely while you turn the handle of the reel. Too much tension will not only foul up your line, but it can also warp your spool. Don't overfill unless you enjoy undoing backlashes. But don't underfill either. A lunker needs plenty of room to run.

A new twist to spoon fishing: Replace the rubber skirt or pork rind on your spoon with a twin-tailed plastic grub body. The two leglike appendages of the grub give the spoon an added lifelike swimming motion and often entice the lunkers to strike. Use colors that contrast with the spoon, according to Mel Anson, an Orlando fisherman who uses this method of angling successfully.

Check your fishing line: Before each trip, check your line for frays and knicks. At the end of each trip, cut at least 10 feet of line from the terminal end. Also, if you use suntan oil or lotion during your fishing trip, wash your hands thoroughly. Some oils tend to weaken fishing line. At home, do not store your reels where it's hot. Heat weakens the line, too.

Keep a bar of soap in your boat.

Take a flashlight along: A flashlight or spotlight may not be as effective as a flare, but it can be a good signaling device if you get stranded. Keep one aboard and remember the international distress SOS signal: three short flashes followed by three longer flashes, followed by three more short flashes. Mirrors are also good signaling devices on sunny days.

Surface lure action: How long should you let a topwater lure lie motionless on the water surface after casting it? Most veterans advise that you let the lure lie still for 10 to 12 seconds before starting your retrieve. Give the lure a small twitch before starting the regular retrieve.

From small ponds to big lakes: When fishing small lakes, remember bass can be lurking anywhere from shallow-water weedy cover to deep-water holes. Use more than one lure and take the time to fish each bush, tree and weed pocket. Use spinnerbaits, plastic worms and minnow-type lures. When fishing large lakes, use the same techniques but concentrate on a specific area and fish it thoroughly.

For the little ones: To make a fishing outing a great experience for kids, remember to keep them comfortable. Take along the sunscreen, some snacks, cool drinks and insect repellent. Start a child on spincasting equipment and try to fish near an area where there are panfish, virtually guaranteeing a fish or two.

6

FISHING IN
NORTHWEST FLORIDA

The Florida Game and Fresh Water Fish Commission divides the state into five regions: Northwest, Northeast, Central, South and the Everglades. Included in chapters dealing with each region are public ramps, fish camps and accommodations offered, the kinds of fish found in each region and the best months to fish for them.

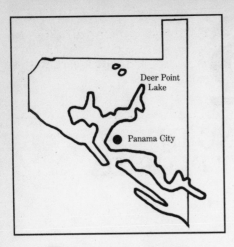

BAY COUNTY

Deer Point Lake: Fed by a natural freshwater stream, this 5,000-acre lake is near Panama City off U.S. Highway 231 and State Road 77 at Southport. Shellcracker fishing is good April through June — that is also the best time to catch redears. Earthworms are the best bait, but fly fishing is also good in the early morning and late afternoon. Bluegill fishing is also good in the spring. Use live crickets or earthworms. Bass fishing is best from spring to early summer and again in the fall. Use plastic worms and crankbaits. Broken-back minnow lures also are effective when fished near the shoreline.

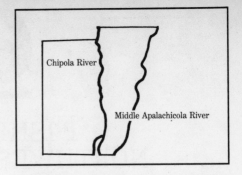

CALHOUN COUNTY

Chipola River: Home of the rare Coosa bass, this river is accessible at Marianna via U.S. Highway 90, State Road 20 at Clarksville and S.R. 274 west of Altha. This scenic cold-water river is spring fed and has fast-water shoals. It offers excellent bream fishing, including bluegill and redbreast. Use Beetle Spins and redworms. Crickets are good, too. Some bass will hit plastic worms in the spring.

Middle Apalachicola River (Blountstown area): Tributaries include Old River, Outside Lakes, Equaloxic Creek, Larkin Slough, River Styx, Kennedy Creek and many other sloughs and streams. The river can be reached over S.R. 20 at Blountstown. Bluegill and shellcracker fishing is excellent in the spring around fallen or submerged treetops and in sloughs off the river. Best baits are crickets, earthworms, catalpa worms and oak worms. Bass fishing is superb in the spring and summer. Anglers should use plastic worms and crankbaits. White and sunshine bass will hit in the spring and fall off sandbars. Use jigs, spoons or live shad. Speckled perch will hit from January through March around fallen treetops. Use live minnows for best results.

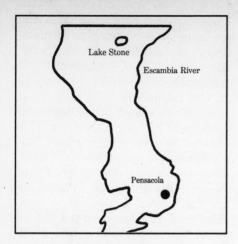

ESCAMBIA COUNTY

Escambia River: The river flows out of south Alabama into Escambia Bay. Some popular access points are Century, McDavid, Molino and the U.S. Highway 90 crossing. Bluegill and shellcracker fishing is best here in the spring near the delta area. Use earthworms. Fly fishing for bream is good in the spring. Bass fishing is good in the delta area in the spring and fall. Use crankbaits for best results, but live shrimp will entice bass to the hook during the summer months in the delta. Sunshine bass fishing is also good in this area during the summer. Late summer is best for largemouths and sunshines. Sunshine bass hit live shrimp, jigs and spoons. For speckled perch, try fishing around fallen treetops and sloughs in January and February. Use live minnows.

Stone Lake: This 130-acre lake near Century is a fish management area limed and fertilized by the game and fish commission to increase fish production. Panfishing for bream is good in the spring. Use live crickets and earthworms. Bass fishing is best in the spring and early summer. Topwater lures and dark-colored plastic worms are good bass lures. Fish

these lures at daylight and late afternoon for best action. Catfish have been stocked and will hit earthworms or chicken livers.

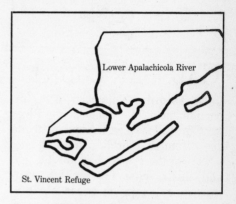

FRANKLIN COUNTY

Lower Ochlockonee River and Lower Apalachicola River: See Gulf and Liberty counties

St. Vincent Refuge: This 12,350-acre island 5 miles offshore from Apalachicola is accessible only by boat. Primitive freshwater fishing areas can be reached from the island's east shoreline. Fishermen will need to carry a small boat for portaging when necessary. Bream and bass fishing is excellent in the spring. Best baits are crickets and earthworms. Bass are more likely to hit plastic worms and live shiners. For more information and a map of the area, write to the St. Vincent Wildlife Refuge, P.O. Box 447, Apalachicola, Fla. 32320, or call (904) 653-8808. According to the U.S. Fish and Wildlife Service, the refuge is temporarily closed because of hurricane damage, and may reopen in the spring of 1988.

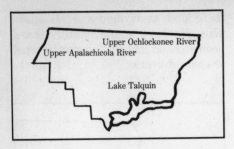

GADSDEN COUNTY

Lake Talquin: This 8,850-acre impoundment on the Ochlockonee River west of Tallahassee is reputed to be one of North Florida's finest fishing lakes. Spring is excellent for bluegill and shellcracker fishing. Use redworms, crickets or grass shrimp. Also, fly fishing is good for bream during early morning and late afternoon hours. Spring is the best time for bass fishing and the fishing is excellent during that time. Some good areas for the largemouths are the creeks and channels on the upper end of the lake. The best baits are crankbaits, plastic worms and surface lures. Live shiners are good for trophy bass. Although the lake is not noted for its speck fishing, some good strings are caught during January and February on live minnows. Striped bass fishing is good — and there are plenty of stripers in Lake Talquin. Best times are spring and fall. Use deep-diving minnow-type lures for best results. In the fall look for diving birds, a sure sign of stripers schooling. The feeding stripers will push the shad to the surface where birds dive for them. Toss a plug into the school and hang on for some heavy action.

Upper Apalachicola River: This covers from Lake Seminole to Blountstown and includes tailwaters below the reservoir at Chattahoochee. It can be reached over U.S. Highway 90 at Chattahoochee, over S.R. 20 at Blountstown and off S.R. 69 and over sand roads leading to the river. This river offers great sunshine bass fishing during the spring and fall. Many state records have been caught below the Jim Woodruff Dam. Best baits are jigs, spoons and live shad. Sunshine bass often school on the surface in the fall and anglers can take limits in minutes when using spoons. White bass fishing is good in March on crayfish and grass shrimp fished on bottom. Bluegill and redbreast fishing is best during the spring on crickets, earthworms and catalpa worms (taken from catalpa trees when they are feeding on the leaves). The shellcrackers hit best on live earthworms around the race shoal area. Bass fishing for largemouths is good in the spring and early summer on plastic worms and crankbaits. There is fair striper fishing in the spring and fall. Best baits in the fall include small live eels fished off the Jim Woodruff Dam catwalk. Deep-diving lures are also effective. Use the ones that resemble minnows.

GULF COUNTY

Dead Lakes: Located in both Gulf and Calhoun counties, this 6,700-acre lake is on the Chipola River near the town of Wewahitchka. Its dark water is filled with cypress trees, snags and stumps. The lake has a reputation for its bluegill and shellcracker fishing. Use earthworms for shellcrackers and live crickets or earthworms for bluegills. Fish among the cypress trees. Largemouth bass fishing is good in the spring and fall on plastic worms and broken-back minnow lures.

Lake Wimico: This is a 4,055-acre natural lake accessible only by boat via the Intracoastal Waterway from Apalachicola or White City. Freshwater and saltwater species of fish are intermixed in these waters. This wide, shallow lake has good bluegill and shellcracker fishing in the spring and early summer. Best baits are crickets and earthworms. Some bass hit artificial worms and crankbaits during spring and early summer.

Lower Apalachicola River: (Delta section) Numerous sloughs and streams, including Brothers River, Howard's Creek, Brickyard Cutoff, Owl Creek and East River, empty into the river. You can reach the river off S.R. 71 at Honeyville, over S.R.

381 to Willis Landing on Brothers River and over U.S. highways 98 and 319 at Apalachicola. Sunshine bass hit during the spring and fall off the sand bars. Best baits include live shad and spoons. Largemouth bass fishing is excellent in the spring on plastic worms and crankbaits. In the summer, good strings of largemouth bass will hit live shrimp fished around the grass flats and canals. Bluegills and shellcrackers hit mostly in the spring on earthworms and crickets. Fly fishing for bream is good during early morning and late afternoon. Some large channel catfish hit in the river channel. Use earthworms or catalpa worms and fish on the bottom.

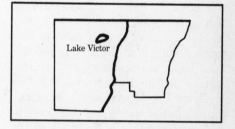

HOLMES COUNTY

Lake Victor: This 130-acre management area near New Hope Community off S.R. 2 is known primarily as a bass lake because some trophy bass have been caught here. Shiners seem to catch the trophy bass, but artificial worms and crankbaits also are recommended for good catches. Spring and early summer are the best times. Bream fishing is good from mid-May to July on earthworms and crickets. Channel catfish will hit earthworms and catalpa worms fished on bottom in the river channel. Chicken livers also work well for catfish.

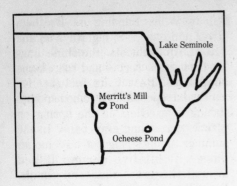

JACKSON COUNTY

Lake Seminole: This 37,500-acre impoundment near Chattahoochee is also called the Jim Woodruff Dam. There are 8,000 acres on the Florida side; the rest is in Georgia. Easy access is available along S.R. 271 north of Sneads. Bank fishing is popular in this area. Sunshine and striped bass fishing is a good bet in this lake that yielded a former record striper. The prime fishing is in the spring and the best baits are spinners and plastic worms as the bass move into the shallows. For bluegill and shellcracker, fish in the spring and use crickets and earthworms. Fly fishing is excellent for bream when the mayflies hatch and fall into the lake. Some large strings of speckled perch are caught in January and February on live minnows.

Merritt's Mill Pond: Near the Marianna city limits, this 202-acre impoundment has spring-fed crystal clear waters. This is one of the top shellcracker fishing spots in the state. Both bluegill and shellcracker fishing is good with earthworms and light tackle. Catalpa worms are also good for bluegills. Because of the clear water, you need light line and tackle when fishing for bass. Live shiners and plastic worms are good for bass angling. A state record shellcracker that weighed more than 4 pounds was caught here. Overcast days are the most productive. Rain or a slight ripple on the water enhances fishing in this pond.

Ocheese Pond: This 2,235-acre pond south of U.S. Highway 90 at Grand Ridge and Sneads offers some big bream and bass. Hand-size bream hit in the spring and prefer grass shrimp. Crickets and earthworms are the next choices. Bass fishing is good in the spring and early summer. Live shiners are excellent bait. Surface lures are good also when fished at dawn and dusk. Some big warmouths can be caught around the base of cypress trees in the spring and summer on earthworms.

JEFFERSON COUNTY

Aucilla River: A cold spring-fed stream on U.S. highways 27 and 98 southeast of Tallahassee, this river has some excellent bream fishing in the spring. Use Beetle Spins and redworms and fish near the shoreline. For largemouth bass, fish near the shoreline during the spring and use artificial worms.

Lake Miccosukee: This 6,226-acre impoundment is east of Tallahassee in Jefferson and Leon counties. Travel on U.S. Highway 90 and S.R. 59 near the town of Miccosukee. The lake offers plenty of bluegills in the spring on crickets and redworms. The best bass fishing is in the spring and the most popular baits are spinnerbaits and artificial worms.

Wacissa River: Noted for its clear water, wild beauty and winding course through tall cypress trees, this cold-water stream is a favorite for canoe trips and float fishing. Access is from S.R. 59 at the town of Wacissa. The best bass fishing is during the spring and summer months. Best lures are artificial worms. Bream fishing is fair on worms and live crickets.

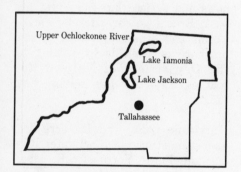

LEON COUNTY

Lake Iamonia: This 5,757-acre lake is almost entirely covered with vegetation. About 12 miles north of Tallahassee, it can be reached by U.S. Highway 319 and S.R. 12. It is noted for its large panfish. Bluegills can be caught in the spring and early summer on oakworms, earthworms and crickets. Pickerels hit best in the spring on broken-back artificial lures that resemble minnows and also on spinnerbaits. Bass fishing is just fair.

Lake Jackson: This 4,004-acre lake near Tallahassee on U.S. Highway 27 is one of Florida's top bass fishing lakes and as such produces large bass throughout the year. The best time to fish for bass is in the spring and the best bait is live shiners. Artificial worms are also effective for bass. Bluegill and shellcracker fishing is best in the spring on grass shrimp and earthworms. Some good strings of speckled perch are caught in the late winter by anglers drift fishing with live minnows.

Upper Ochlockonee River: (From Florida-Georgia line to Lake Talquin). The river can be reached via U.S. highways 90 and 27 and S.R. 12. Some upper stretches of the river are difficult for boat travel because of logs and brush jams during low water. This is the only system in northwest Florida known to support Suwannee bass. Bluegill and shellcracker fishing is excellent in the spring and summer months on crickets, redworms and wigglers. Bass hit best in the spring and summer on crankbaits and artificial worms. Lures are more effective when fished around the many logs and fallen treetops in the river.

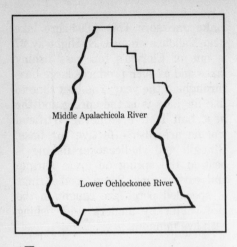

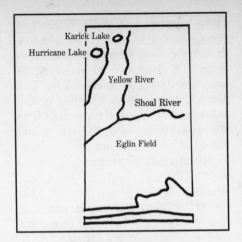

LIBERTY COUNTY

Lower Ochlockonee River: (Southward from Jackson Bluff Dam, also known as Lake Talquin Dam on S.R. 20 to Ochlockonee Bay) It can also be reached off S.R. 375 to Sopchoppy and S.R. 67 southward from Telogia. Striped bass fishing is good periodically in the fall and early spring. Live shad are the best bait to use right below the Talquin Dam. Bluegill and shellcracker fishing is excellent in the spring. Best baits are redworms, wigglers and crickets. Bass fishing can be productive in the spring and early summer on crankbaits and plastic worms when fished near fallen treetops and logs.

OKALOOSA COUNTY

Eglin Field: Numerous artificial and natural ponds, natural lakes and creeks are located here. Spring is the best time to fish for bass or bream. Artificial worms, broken-back minnows and surface lures are best for bass. Bream go for crickets, earthworms and grass shrimp. A fishing brochure is available by writing to the Department of Natural Resources, Eglin Air Force Base, Fla. 32542.

Hurricane Lake: This 350-acre fish management lake in Blackwater River State Forest north of S.R. 4 between Baker and Munson offers camping facilities as well as good fishing for large bass. The best baits for bass are either green or black artificial worms. Fish them in the spring and early summer for best results. Bream fishing is fair in the spring on crickets and earthworms. Catfish have been stocked and can be caught on earthworms and chicken livers. Fish on the bottom for catfish.

Karick Lake: A 58-acre fish management area near Blackman off S.R. 189, this lake also offers camping sites on both sides of the lake. It is an outstanding lake for bluegills in the spring and early summer. Catfish have been stocked here also and will hit earthworms or chicken livers fished on bottom. Bass fishing is good in the spring on artificial worms and spinnerbaits.

Shoal River: This river can be reached by U.S. Highway 90, 4 miles east of Crestview and S.R. 85, 5 miles south of Crestview. The best fishing is in the lower section of the river. Spring and summer are best for both bass and bream. Some large bass are caught on crankbaits and plastic worms. Jigger fishing is good for bass in the murky water. For bream use crickets and earthworms. Fly fishing for bream is also good in the early morning and late afternoon.

Yellow River: This river has 50 miles of swift-running, yellow-brown water. It can be reached by U.S. Highway 90 at Milligan, S.R. 2 at Oak Grove in Okaloosa County, and S.R. 87 in Santa Rosa County. The lower reaches of the river are best for fishing. Spring and summer are the best times to catch bluegills and shellcrackers. The best baits are redworms, wigglers and crickets. Bass fishing is productive in the spring on crankbaits and artificial worms.

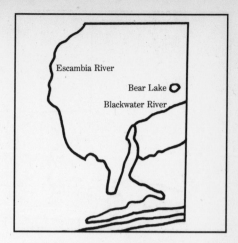

SANTA ROSA COUNTY

Bear Lake: A 107-acre fish management area in Blackwater River State Forest off S.R. 4 east of Munson, this lake has excellent bluegill fishing. Camping facilities are also top-notch. Spring is the best time to catch bass and bream. Artificial worms are best for bass and earthworms and crickets are best for bream. Catfish have been stocked and can be caught best while bottom fishing with earthworms or chicken livers.

Blackwater River: There are excellent sites for camping and picnicking along this stream, which can be reached at Milton on U.S. Highway 90. Several of the stretches are too shallow for motorboats during the dry seasons. The lower section of the river provides the best fishing. Bluegills and redbreast sunfish hit in the spring and early summer on Beetle Spins, crickets and earthworms. Bass fishing is fair in the spring. Best baits are artificial worms and crankbaits.

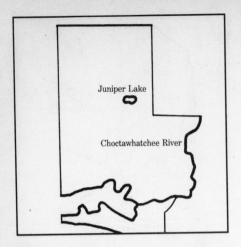

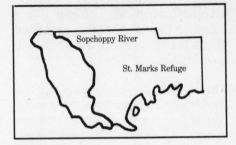

weedless Texas Rig with enough lead to get the lure down into the brush. Live shiners work well also. Bluegills hit best in the spring and summer on crickets and wigglers.

WALTON COUNTY

Choctawhatchee River: This stream flows 96 miles from the Alabama line to Choctawhatchee Bay. Popular access points are Caryville, Ebro and Black Creek south of Freeport. The river offers alligator gar fishing in season with some of these heavy-weights tipping the scales at 200 pounds. Anglers catch good strings of bluegills and shellcrackers on the lower river during the spring and summer. Although crickets and earthworms are good panfish baits, fly fishing is exciting during the spring and summer. Largemouth bass hit best in the spring and summer on crankbaits and artificial worms. Fish around fallen treetops and practically anything sticking up out of the river. Sunshine bass fishing is spotty in the spring and fall. Use live shad and shadlike artificial lures and fish on the downstream end of the sand bars.

Juniper Lake: A 670-acre fish management area 3 miles north of De-Funiak Springs west of S.R. 83, this impoundment has lots of flooded timber and produces some excellent bass fishing. A number of trophy bass are taken each year from this lake. Plastic worms are the best because of underwater trees and snags. Use a

WAKULLA COUNTY

Sopchoppy River: This is the tributary to the lower Ochlockonee River in Wakulla County and can be reached from U.S. Highway 319 south of the town of Sopchoppy. Bream fishing is good for bluegills and shellcrackers during the spring and summer months on crickets, red-worms and wigglers. Bass fishing is fair during spring and summer on broken-back minnows and artificial worms.

St. Marks Refuge: Located in Wakulla, Jefferson and Taylor counties, the St. Marks Refuge can be reached via U.S. Highway 319 at several state road junctions at Wakulla, Crawford-ville, Sopchoppy, Newport and Panacea. Bream and bass fishing is good in the spring. According to the U.S. Fish and Wildlife Service, the ponds are open year-round for bank fishing. To protect migratory waterfowl, boats are not allowed from Oct. 15 to March 15. For more information, write to St. Marks Refuge Manager, P.O. Box 68, St. Marks, Fla. 32355.

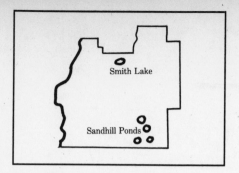

WASHINGTON COUNTY

Sandhill Ponds: These "ponds" are natural lakes that range in size from 200 to 400 acres. Some of the larger ones are Crystal Lake, Porter, Gap, Hammock, Hamilton, Wages, Dunford, Hicks, Lucas, Pate and Rattlesnake ponds. These lakes are not limited to Washington County — they extend into Bay County also. Fringed with cypress trees, they are clear, deep, cold-water lakes. Access is by ungraded and unmarked sand roads. All of the lakes can be reached in both Washington and Bay counties on upgraded roads off S.R. 77 between Chipley and Panama City. These ponds offer good bass and bream fishing in the spring and summer. Bass hit smaller artificial worms (not longer than 6 inches). Bream prefer crickets and earthworms.

Smith Lake: This 160-acre lake is 3 miles south of Bonifay off S.R. 79. It is a cypress bay lake with very dark tannin-stained water. The lower end of the lake was rejuvenated in 1977 and now offers improved bank fishing areas. Bream fishing is popular from early spring through late summer. Because of aquatic vegetation and cypress trees, bass anglers prefer spinnerbaits and artificial worms. However, live shiners are productive in open areas. Wigglers and crickets are favorites of bream fishermen.

NORTHWEST FLORIDA FISH CAMPS

BAY COUNTY

Deer Point Lake

Cedar Creek Bait Ranch:
Resota Beach Road.
Route 4, Box 695, Panama City, 32405;(904) 265-9587.
Bait, tackle, gas, groceries and ice.

Deer Point Dam Bait & Tackle
3610 Co. Rd. 2321, Panama City, 32404; (904) 763-1494.
Bait, tackle, groceries.

Tharp's Camp Cedar:
End of Resota Beach Road.
Route 4, Box 737, Panama City, 32405;(904) 265-2330.
Ramp, boats, motors, bait, ice, tackle, groceries, gas, licenses, overnight living units, campsites.

Bear Creek

Cherokee Landing
Co. Rd. 2301 at Bear Creek bridge crossing.
Route A, Box 209D, Youngstown, 32466; (904) 722-4902.
Ramp, boats, canoes, bait, tackle, snacks, licenses, camping, hunting supplies, RV park.

Cox Fish Camp:
First right after crossing Bear Creek Bridge on Co. Rd. 2301.
Route A, Box 180, Youngstown, 32466; (904) 722-4441.
Private ramp, bait, boats and camping.

Econfina Creek

Econfina Creek Canoe Livery:
One mile north of Highway 20 on Strickland Road.
Route B, Box 1570, Youngstown, 32466; (904) 722-9032
Public ramp, canoes, bait, ice, primitive campsites, bathhouse and fishing guide service.

CALHOUN COUNTY

Chipola River

Tucker's Bait and Grocery:
Scott's Ferry on S.R. 71.
Route 1, Box 99, Blountstown, 32424; 904/674-8290.
Private ramp, bait, tackle, ice, groceries and campgrounds.

ESCAMBIA COUNTY

Escambia River

Smith's Fish Camp:
U.S. Highway 90 at Escambia River Bridge about 10 miles northeast of Pensacola.
(904) 476-3353.
Private ramp, boats, bait, tackle and groceries. No living units.

FRANKLIN COUNTY

Apalachicola River

Bay City Lodge:
State Road 384 at Apalachicola.
P.O. Box 172, Apalachicola, 32320; (904) 653-9294.
Private ramp, boats, motors, bait, ice, groceries, guides. Restaurant and living units.

Breakaway Lodge:
200 Waddell Road, Apalachicola, 32320; (904) 653-8897.
Private ramp, boats, motors, gas, bait, tackle, ice, groceries, guides and licenses. Restaurant and lounge, motel units and campsites.

Sportsmen's Lodge:
400 yards north of U.S. Highway 98 on Apalachicola Bay, east of the bridge.
P.O. Box 606, Eastpoint, 32328; (904) 670-8423.
Private ramp, gas, bait, tackle, ice, guide service, living units, public ramp available nearby.

GADSDEN COUNTY

Lake Talquin

Ingram's Marina:
Off State Road 267, 13 miles south of Quincy.
Route 3, Box 2769, Quincy, 32351; (904) 627-2241.
Bait, tackle, cabins, public ramp, groceries, boats for rent, licenses, trailer hookup and guides.

Whippoorwill Marina:
Off State Road 267, 10 miles south of Quincy.
(904) 627-3854.
Boats, tackle, bait, groceries.

Idlewilde Fishing Lodge:
Highway 65-C off State Road 267, 8 miles south of Quincy.
Route 3, Quincy, 32351; (904) 627-3589.
Private ramps, boats and campers for rent, bait, tackle.

Gainey's Talquin Lodge:
On Highway 65-C off State Road 267, 8 miles south of Quincy.
Route 3, Box 1607, Quincy, 32351; (904) 627-3822.
Restaurant, cabins, bait, tackle, boats for rent, motel, camper hook-ups, guides, licenses.

Robinson Fish Camp:
Off State Road 267 on Highway 65-C. Route 3, Box 1540, Quincy, 32351
(904) 627-3479.
Boats, bait, tackle.

Lake Seminole/Apalachicola River

Sportsman Inn:
Junction of Lake Seminole and Apalachicola River (near Jim Woodruff Dam).
516 W. Washington St., Chattahoochee, 32324; (904) 663-4026 or (904) 663-2352.
Motel and kitchenette units, battery hook-ups (for boat battery charges), guide service for Lake Seminole and Apalachicola River.

GULF COUNTY

Chipola River

Douglas Landing Trading Post:
Highway 71 South from Wewahitchka, left on C-381, 4.5 miles east of Highway 71.
P.O. Box 262, Wewahitchka, 32465; (904) 639-5481.
Bait, beverages, ice, groceries, gas, oil, licenses, full RV facilities, campgrounds, hot showers and private boat ramps.

Dead Lakes State Park and Recreation Area:
P.O. Box 989, Wewahitchka, 32465; (904) 639-2702.

Howard's Creek

Howard's Creek Boat Landing, Lower Landing:
91 Duval, Port St. Joe, 32456; (904) 229-8389.
Private launching facilities, camping facilities (tent and RV).

Depot Creek

Public Ramp:
7.5 miles east of Port St. Joe on Highway 98. Turn north at Odena Fire Tower.
Public boat ramp to Depot Creek and access to Lake Wimico.

Dead Lakes

Gates Fish Camp:
4 miles east of Wewahitchka on SR 71.
Route 3 Box 279, Wewahitchka, 32465; (904) 639-2768.
Licenses, tackle, bait, boats, motors, camping facilities and cabins.

Cypress Lodge:
Off Highway 71, 4 miles north of Wewahitchka.
Route 3, Box 172-A, Wewahitchka, 32465; (904) 639-5414.
Private ramp, boats, licenses, motors, bait, tackle, cabins and restaurant.

Lake Side Lodge:
One mile north of Wewahitchka on Highway 71.
P.O. Box 1069, Wewahitchka, 32465; (904) 639-2681.
Private ramp, boats, motors, bait, tackle and hunting supplies.

Fisher's Bait and Tackle:
At Dead Lakes Dam.
Route 2, Box 2095, Wewahitchka, 32465; (904) 639-5051.
Private ramp on Dead Lakes and private ramp on Chipola Cutoff, camping facilities, cottages with cooking facilities, boats, licenses, groceries, bait, tackle and hunting supplies.

HOLMES COUNTY

Lake Victor

Riddle's Bait and Tackle Shop:
Off S.R. 2.
Route 1 Box 279 Westville, 32464; (904) 956-2444.
Public ramps, campsites.

JACKSON COUNTY

Lake Seminole

Paramore Restaurant:
North of Sneads on S.R. 271.
Route 1, Box 78A, Sneads, 32460; (904) 592-2091.
Public ramp, ice, restaurant and camping.

Seminole Lodge:
Off U.S. Hwy. 90 at Sneads, over Legion Road.
Route 1, Box 17B, Sneads, 32460; (904) 593-6886.
Private ramps, boats, bait, ice, gas, licenses, overnight living units, groceries, tackle and RV hookups.

Cooleys Fishing Camp:
4 miles north of Sneads on S.R. 271.
Route 1 Box 17B, Sneads, 32460; (904) 593-6935.
Public ramp, bait, ice, groceries, tackle, licenses, overnight living units and campsites, boat rental, pawn shop.

Merritt's Mill Pond

Hasty's Fishing Camp:
S.R. 164 off U.S Hwy. 71, 5 miles east of Marianna.
Route 8, Box 655, Marianna, 32446; (904) 482-5545.
Private ramps, boats, motors, tackle, gas, groceries, bait, licenses, campsites, fishing dock.

LEON COUNTY

Lake Jackson

Red and Sam's Fish Camp:
U.S. 27 north of Tallahassee.
5563 North Monroe Street, Tallahassee, 32303; (904) 562-3083.
Public ramp, ice, snacks, tackle, bait, guides, licenses, overnight living units and campsites.

Lake Jackson Fishing Lodge:
Lake Drive, east of U.S. 27, off Old Rainbridge Road, north of Tallahasse.
Route 9, Box 83, Tallahassee, 32303; (904) 562-5590.
Paved public ramp, campsite, motor home hook-ups, bait, tackle, ice, boats, motors, guides, licenses, overnight living units, snacks, beverages, oyster bar.

Lake Iamonia

Reeve's Lake Iamonia Landing:
Lake Iamonia Road off S.R. 12 off U.S. 319, north of Tallahassee.
Route 1 Box 662, Tallahassee, 32312; (904) 893-0361.
Public ramps, boats, motors, bait, tackle, groceries, licenses.

Lake Miccosukee

Reeve's Fish Camp:
East from Miccosukee to Magnolia Road, left on Reeve's Landing Road, right to lake.
Route 7 Box 1105, Tallahassee, 32308; (904) 893-9940.
Paved ramp, boats, motors, campsites, bait, tackle, ice, groceries, beverages, licenses, motor home hook-ups, overnight living units, showers.

Lake Talquin
(also see Gadsden County)

Coe's Landing:
West of Tallahassee on Coe's Landing Road off S.R. 20.
Star Route 2, Box 9064, Tallahassee, 32304; (904) 576-5590.
County paved ramp, camping area, boats, motors, 5 camping hook-ups, bait, ice, tackle, groceries and boat storage.

Blount's Camp:
West of Tallahassee on Blount Road off S.R. 20.
Star Route 1, Box 3335, Tallahassee, 32304; (904) 576-4301.
Paved ramp, boats, campsites without hook-ups, overnight living units with kitchens and air conditioning, boat storage.

R.C. Davis Fish Camp:
Davis Road off S.R. 20.
Star Route 1, Box 4013, Tallahassee, 32304;
(904) 576-6303.
Cement ramp, boats, campsites with electricity and water.

LIBERTY COUNTY

Florida River

Florida River Fish Camp:
S.R. 379 south of Bristol.
Route 1, Box 213A, Bristol, 32321; (904) 643-5745.
Private ramp, plug-ins for campers and campsites.

Kennedy Creek

Kennedy Creek Fish Camp:
S.R. 379 south of Bristol.
P.O. Box 145, Sumatra, 32335; (904) 670-8222.
Private ramp, boats, cabins leased by day, week, month and year. Campground and plug-ins for campers.

Ochlockonee River

Ed and Bernice's:
On S.R. 20, below Lake Talquin Dam.
Star Route, Box 1910-C, Tallahassee, 32304;
(904) 379-8122 or (904) 379-8435.
Private ramp, boats, motors, bait, ice, groceries, gas, tackle, licenses, overnight trailer spaces w/ patios and tables.

Richbourg's:
On County Road 333, south of Bristol.
Route 1, Box 115A, Bristol, 32321; (904) 643-5689.
Private boat ramp.

SANTA ROSA COUNTY

Escambia River

Jim's Fish Camp:
U.S. 90 on Escambia Fill.
Route 5, Box 3, Pace, 32571; (904) 994-7500.
Bait and tackle.

Yellow River

Brown's Fish Camp:
S.R. 89 7 miles south of Milton.
Route 4, Box 30, Milton, 32570; (904) 623-6102.
Public ramp and boats. Living units and camper spaces, boat stall rentals.

Couey's Fish Camp:
6 miles south of U.S. 90 east of Milton.
Route 4, Box 31, Milton, 32570; (904) 623-6164.
Public ramp, living units.

WALTON COUNTY

Black Creek

Black Creek Lodge:
Off U.S. 331 near Freeport. Access to Black Creek and Choctawhatchee River Basin and Bay.
Route 2, Box 302, Freeport, 32439;
(904) 835-2541.
Ramp, boats, motors, gas, bait, tackle, cabins, camper-trailer park and showers.

McDaniel's Fish Camp:
At Mitchel River and Black Creek. Access to Choctawhatchee River and Bay.
Route 2, Box 255, Freeport, 32439;
(904) 835-2009.
Ramp.

Juniper Lake

Juniper Lake Campground:
2½ miles north of DeFuniak Springs off U.S. 83.
Route 8, Box 246, DeFuniak Springs, 32433;
(904) 892-3445.
Campsites, trailers, boat rentals, bait and tackle, private boat dumping station, launching, ice, groceries, licenses, dock fishing, and boat fishing.

Kings and Holley Lake

Kings Lake Campground:
4 miles north of DeFuniak Springs off U.S. 331.
Route 5, Box 120C-9, DeFuniak Springs, 32433; (904) 892-7229.
Campsites, cabins, bait, tackle, licenses and boat launching.

Lake Holley/Kings Lake Resort:
About 4 miles north of DeFuniak Springs on U.S. 331.
Route 5, Box 79K, DeFuniak Springs, 32433;
(904) 892-5914.
Campsites, cabins, licenses, bait and tackle, groceries, private boat launch, pool.

Alaqua Creek

Alaqua Landing:
2 miles west of Freeport on S.R. 20. Access to Choctawhatchee Bay.
Route 1, Box 235, Freeport, 32439;
(904) 835-9890.
Public boat launch, bait and tackle.

WAKULLA COUNTY

Ochlockonee River

Bayside Marina:
S.R. 372, Panacea.
P.O. Box 97, Panacea, 32346; (904) 984-5548.
Forklift ramp without backside, boat storage, bait and tackle.

Jack Langston's Place:
S.R. 375, 61 miles south of S.R. 20.
Star Route 1, Box 1373, Tallahassee, 32304; (904) 962-2003
Private ramps, boats, overnight living units by reservation only.

Ochlocknee River State Park:
U.S. 319, Sopchoppy
P.O. Box 5, Sopchoppy, 32358; (904) 962-2771
Public ramp, camping, swimming, skiing, canoeing, and hiking.

McKenzie's Silver Lake:
S.R. 375, 7 miles west of Sopchoppy.
P.O. Box 241, Sopchoppy, 32358; (904) 962-2767.
Private ramp, camping, bathroom facilities, park and RV.

Ted Roberts and Son:
S.R. 375 off S.R. 20.
Star Route, Box 150, Tallahassee, 32304; (904) 962- 4923.
Private ramp.

Wood Lake:
S.R. 375, Apalachicola National Forest.
Public ramp, camping.

St. Marks River

Fort San Marcos County Ramp:
St. Marks.
Public ramp.

Newport County Ramp:
U.S. 98, Newport.
Public ramp.

Shields Marina:
S.R. 363 (U.S. 98).
P.O. Box 218, St. Marks, 32355; (904) 925-6158.
Private ramp, boat service, bait and tackle.

Sopchoppy River

Sopchoppy City Park:
U.S. 319, Sopchoppy.
Public ramp, camping.

Wakulla River

Public ramp on U.S. 98

Shell Island Fish Camp:
St. Marks.
P.O. Box 115 St. Marks, 32355; (904) 925-6398.
Fresh and salt-water fishing. Wet and dry storage, public ramps, boats, motors, bait, tackle, ice, groceries, overnight living units and campsites.

Upper Bridge County Ramp:
Public ramp on U.S. 365.

WASHINGTON COUNTY

Choctawhatchee River

Hide-a-while Fish Camp and RV:
S.R. 20 near Ebro.
P.O. Box 14178 Panama City Beach, 32407; (904) 535-2621.
Boat launching, tackle, refreshments, overnight camping, boat rental, bait, two cottages.

Holmes Creek

Cypress Springs Canoe Trail:
2 miles north of Vernon on S.R. 79. First dirt road on right past Vernon Bridge.
P.O. Box 726, Vernon, 32462; (904) 535-2960.
Canoe rentals, soft drinks and campsites with water and electricity.

NORTHWEST FLORIDA FISHING BAROMETER

Month	Largemouth Bass	Speckled perch	Sunshine bass	Bream
January	Poor	Excellent	Poor	Poor
February	Good	Excellent	Good	Fair
March	Excellent	Good	Excellent	Good
April	Excellent	Fair	Excellent	Excellent
May	Excellent	Poor	Fair	Excellent
June	Good	Poor	Fair	Excellent
July	Good	Poor	Fair	Good
August	Good	Poor	Good	Good
September	Good	Poor	Good	Good
October	Good	Fair	Good	Good
November	Fair	Fair	Good	Fair
December	Fair	Good	Fair	Poor

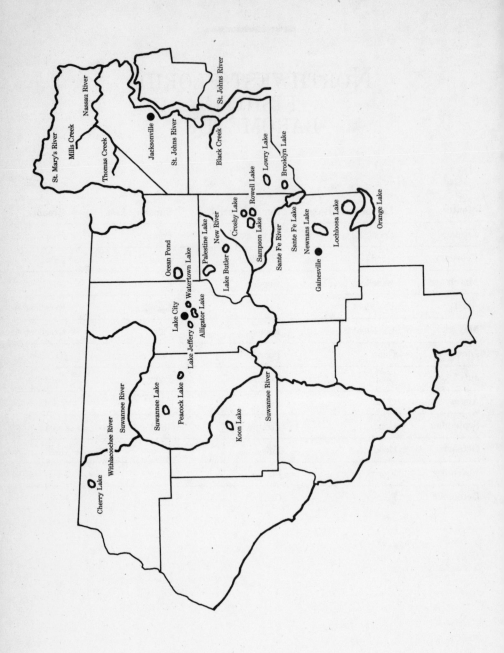

7

FISHING IN NORTHEAST FLORIDA

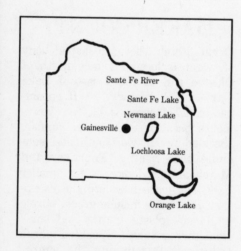

ALACHUA COUNTY

Orange Lake: This 12,700-acre lake is the largest lake in the northeast region. It is a fish management area located 10 miles southeast of Gainesville and offers a wide variety of fishing for speckled perch, bluegills, redears, warmouths and largemouth bass. Fishing for trophy bass weighing more than 10 pounds is excellent during January, February and

March. The most productive baits and lures include live wild shiners, purple and black artificial worms and topwater float-diving lures fished around hydrilla beds. The peak speckled perch season is during February, March and April. Live minnows and minijigs are the top producers, especially when the crappie move into the shoreline areas to spawn. Bluegill and redear fishing is outstanding from April to June. Live shrimp are by far the top producers.

Lochloosa Lake: An 8,000-acre lake, Lochloosa is connected to Orange Lake by Cross Creek. This management area is known for its speckled perch, but also has bluegills, redears and bass. Fishing for trophy bass is excellent during January, February and March. Wild shiners, purple and black plastic worms and topwater float-diving type lures fished around hydrilla beds are the best for catching bass. The peak months for speckled perch are February through April. Live minnows and small jigs are the top producers, especially when the fish move into shallow shoreline water to spawn. Bluegill and redear fishing is outstanding from April through June on grass shrimp. There are four brush-type fish attractors in Lochloosa Lake. Fish attractors are usually brush anchored with concrete blocks.

Newnans Lake: Access to this 5,800-acre lake 1½ miles east of Gainesville is by state roads 20, 26 and 234. The lake provides good largemouth fishing during February and March. Action slows after March. Popular lures include spinnerbaits with a pork frog, blue and purple artificial worms and crankbaits. Speck fishing is productive throughout the year. Most fish are caught with live minnows or by trolling small jigs. Bluegill and redear fishing is good throughout April, May, June and July — also when the water level is high. For best results, fish the cypress tree shoreline with live grass shrimp or live crickets. There are three brush-type fish attractors in this lake. Sunshine bass angling is good from November through March with many of the fish caught by speckled perch fishermen drifting with live minnows. If you want to go strictly for sunshine bass, fish dead shiners on the bottom or use deep-running minnow-type artificial lures.

Santa Fe Lake: Located 1½ miles south of Waldo on U.S. Highway 301 (Earleton Beach) or near Melrose on state roads 26 or 21, this 5,800-acre lake is cypress-lined with extensive grass areas. The lake offers good bass fishing during early spring. After that, fishing declines. Small schooling fish can be caught throughout the year. The best baits for largemouth bass include float-diving lures, purple or black plastic worms and crankbaits. Speck fishing is good dur-

ing February and March. Drift live minnows in open water at a depth of 4 to 5 feet. Bluegill and shellcracker fishing is available, but this lake is not a big producer of bream. Live worms and crickets are usually the favored baits. This lake has five brush-type fish attractors and offers good sunshine bass angling.

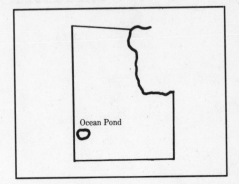
Ocean Pond

BAKER COUNTY

Ocean Pond: This dish-shaped body of water is located 1 mile north of Olustee and 12 miles east of Lake City on U.S. Highway 90. It encompasses 1,774 acres and offers largemouth bass, bluegill, redear sunfish, speckled perch, warmouth and sunshine bass fishing. February and March are good months for smaller bass, but large bass are the exception. Best baits include green, purple and black plastic worms and small float-diving lures. Speckled perch fishing is fair during the winter months. Drift fish with live minnows just off bottom for best results. Bluegill and shellcracker fishing is poor. Crickets and live worms work best. Most fish are taken while drifting with live minnows. Ocean Pond has three brush-type fish attractors.

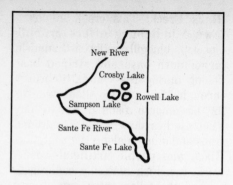

New River

Crosby Lake

Rowell Lake

Sampson Lake

Sante Fe River

Sante Fe Lake

BRADFORD COUNTY

Sampson Lake: A 2,042-acre lake, it is located 4 miles west of Starke off S.R. 100. This lake — an infertile body of water with only three deep holes — offers excellent largemouth bass fishing February through April when the fish move into the maiden-cane, hydrilla and lily pad shoreline to spawn. The best baits for spring fishing are spinnerbaits and purple or blue plastic worms. Crappie (speck) fishing is fair with best months in January, February and March. Drift live minnows near the bottom for best results. Bluegill and shellcracker fishing is excellent during April, May and June when the fish move into the maidencane to spawn. The best baits are worms and crickets. Sunshine bass are a local favorite and provide good action during the winter months. Most fish are taken while speck fishing with minnows. This lake has three brush-type fish attractors.

Rowell Lake: This 363-acre lake is 4 miles west of Starke off S.R. 100. It has a flat, featureless bottom with a maximum depth of 6 feet. Rowell Lake offers excellent largemouth bass fishing from January through June on purple and black plastic worms. Live shiners drifted in open water work well. Artificial lures are most effective cast into the cypress trees along the shoreline. Speck fish-

ing is excellent with the favored bait: live minnows. Drift fish in open water. Bluegills and redears grow at a fast rate in this eutrophic lake and offer some good, scrappy angling. Worms and crickets work best when the fish move into the cypress tree shoreline. The best months are April through June. Fish around the orange and white buoys — they mark the numerous fish attractors in the lake. The winter months are excellent for sunshine bass fishing.

Crosby Lake: Noted for its speckled perch and yearling bass, this 400-acre lake is 1½ miles west of Starke off S.R. 100. While it offers fair bass fishing throughout the year, it rarely yields anything larger than yearlings. The best baits are small float-diving lures and small purple and black plastic worms. Speck fishing can be excellent. For best results, fish around the brush-type fish attractors. Use live minnows in water about 3 feet deep. Bluegill and shellcracker fishing is poor.

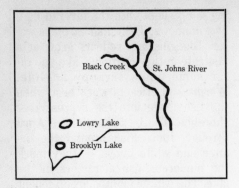

CLAY COUNTY

Brooklyn Lake: This 650-acre lake and Lake Geneva, which has 1,650 acres, are near Keystone Heights on S.R. 100. Both of these infertile lakes offer fair fishing for largemouths November through March. The best baits to use are small topwater lures and small blue or green artificial worms fished near the maidencane along the shoreline or in the deep-water grass beds. Crappie (speck) fishing is fair during the winter. Drift live minnows near the bottom for best results. Bluegill and shellcracker fishing is poor. Brooklyn Lake has one brush-type fish attractor in deep water near a grass bed. Note: There is quite a bit of skiing traffic on the lakes.

Lowry Lake: Four miles north of Keystone Heights on S.R. 21 in the Camp Blanding Wildlife Management Area, this 1,260-acre lake offers good fishing for yearling largemouths January through March when the fish are spawning near the maidencane beds. The most productive lures are small surface lures — the float-diving types are best — and small blue and green artificial worms. Speck fishing is fair when live minnows are drifted near the bottom in open water. May and June are best for bluegills and redears.

Black Creek: This creek in downtown Middleburg offers crappie (specks), bluegill, redbreast sunfish, largemouth bass and striped bass fishing during the winter. February through May are excellent months for largemouth fishing. For trophy bass, use live shiners and fish around trees and stumps along the shoreline. Black and purple artificial worms work, too. Fish normally congregate around the fallen trees and stumps near shore. Redbreast fishing is excellent throughout the summer on live worms and crickets or small spinnerbaits fished near the shoreline. Crappie fishing is fair on small minnows and jigs during February and March.

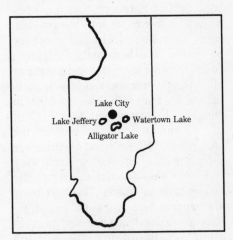

COLUMBIA COUNTY

Watertown Lake: Located on the outskirts of Lake City off S.R. 100-A, this 46-acre lake is a fish management area. While bass can be caught throughout the year, February through April is best for largemouth fishing. The best baits are surface lures and purple, blue and black artificial worms. Speck fishing is fair throughout the year using live minnows in open water. Bluegill fishing is excellent. Most are caught by trolling small spinners in open water or by fishing live crickets near shoreline vegetation.

Alligator Lake: This 338-acre lake in Lake City has largemouth bass, crappie, bluegill and redear sunfish. Largemouth fishing is outstanding during February and March. For best results, use float-diving lures and purple, blue, black and motor-oil colored plastic worms. Crappie fishing is good during March, but is slow the rest of the year. Use live minnows and fish about 3 feet deep in open water. Fish for bluegills April through September using live crickets near vegetation.

Lake Jeffery: This trip will cost you. Admission to the 114-acre lake 3 miles west of Lake City on S.R. 250 is 50 cents a person and there is a $2 charge to launch your boat. Lake Jeffery offers fair bass fishing. Use light line and small lures in this clear-water lake. The best lures are blue, green and cream-colored plastic worms. Speckled perch fishing is fair throughout the year on live minnows. Bluegill fishing is excellent from May through September on live crickets fished near the maidencane beds.

Sante Fe River: Located 17 miles south of Lake City on U.S. highways 41 and 441 at O'Leno State Park, the river offers excellent fishing for Suwannee and largemouth bass. Most bass, however, are in the 1½-pound range or smaller. The combination of swift water and light line will make them feel like 10-pound lunkers. Use small black plastic worms for best results. The best fishing in the river is for redbreast sunfish. This scrappy panfish is caught easily on small spinners, live worms and crickets. Fish near fallen trees or stumps with whatever bait you choose.

DUVAL COUNTY

St. Johns River: Seven miles south of Jacksonville on S.R. 13 and then west on Mills Creek Road about a mile is a river renowned for its largemouth bass fishing. The best baits are purple, blue, black and green plastic worms fished near underwater eel grass beds. Surface lures fished near shoreline stumps can be productive also. Bluegill fishing is excellent around eel grass beds and submerged pilings with live worms, crickets and shrimp fished on bottom.

Hannah Park: (not shown) This 40-acre park is a fish management area — with a nominal admission fee — providing access to a campground and the Atlantic beach. The park has good bass fishing, especially around the small islands in the lake. The best baits are crankbaits and purple, black and blue plastic worms. February, March and April are the best times to catch trophy bass. Bluegill fishing is fair with most in the 7-inch range. Use crickets and live worms and fish on the bottom for best results. The peak season for bluegills is May through July. Sunshine bass also are available and most are caught by fishing on the bottom with dead shrimp.

Pope Duval, St. Augustine Road Ponds, Bethesda Pond, Lee Adams and Oceanway Fish Management Areas: (not shown) These 10- to 20-acre ponds are found throughout the Jacksonville urban area. Fishing is good for bluegills and channel catfish. There are some restrictions on harvesting largemouths.

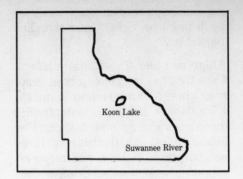

LAFAYETTE COUNTY

Koon Lake: This 110-acre fish management area is 5 miles east of Mayo on U.S. Highway 27 — follow the signs. The lake has a limited bass harvest with most of the fish in the yearling size class. It is heavily infested with underwater vegetation, which makes surface lures the most productive bait to use. Bluegill fishing is fair, but because of vegetation it is hard to fish the lake for bream. Live crickets are the best bait. The peak season for both bass and bluegills is March through May.

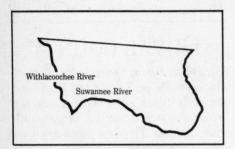

HAMILTON COUNTY

Suwannee River: There are numerous access points to this popular river, which offers excellent largemouth fishing throughout the year for small yearling bass 2 pounds and less. Use small float-diving lures and purple or black plastic worms for best results. Fish around the shoreline and fallen trees or stumps. Redbreast sunfish are by far the most abundant game fish in the river and are easily caught on small spinners fished near fallen trees and stumps. Another good method is to use a long limber cane pole and crickets. Fish along the shoreline as the current takes you downstream. Local anglers call it "throw fishing." Peak season: May through September.

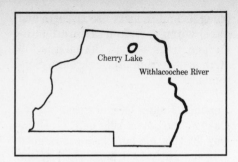

MADISON COUNTY

Cherry Lake: This 479-acre lake is 10 miles north of Madison. Turn right on S.R. 253 for 1½ miles. The lake has excellent bass fishing for the smaller ones; a few 10-pounders are caught each year. Because the water is clear, a light line is a must in this lake. The best baits are blue, green, black and purple artificial worms. The peak season is February through March. Bluegill and shellcracker fishing is fair on live worms and crickets fished on bottom during May, June and July. Sunshine bass, a local favorite, are caught on live shiners or trolled spinners and deep-diving lures from November through February.

Withlacoochee River: Access is available at Blue Springs off S.R. 6. The river offers limited success for largemouth bass on small black or purple worms fished near shoreline cover. The peak season is February through May. Redbreast sunfish can be caught near fallen trees and stumps from March through September on small spinners or crickets.

Suwannee River: There are numerous access points to the Suwannee. It offers excellent largemouth bass fishing throughout the year for small yearling bass 2 pounds and less. Use small float-diving lures or plastic worms — black or purple is best. Fish near the shoreline and around fallen trees or stumps. Redbreast sunfish are the most plentiful fish in the river and are easily caught on small spinners fished near fallen trees and stumps. Another effective method is to use a long, limber cane pole and crickets and fish along the shoreline as the boat drifts downstream. Peak season: May through September.

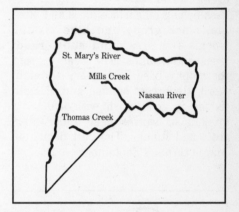

NASSAU COUNTY

Nassau River: This river, which is accessible at the U.S. Highway 17 bridge south of Yulee, offers excellent striped bass fishing December through May. Largemouth bass, bluegill and redbreast sunfish angling is limited. The best bait is live eels fished near the bridge pilings or submerged trees. Another good method is to use saltwater deep-diving lures on falling tides.

St. Mary's River: Boulogne, Macclenny and Hilliard offer access to this river. Largemouth bass, bluegill and redear sunfish can be caught in the river with small bass offering the best fishing. For best bass results, use surface lures and small black or purple plastic worms fished near fallen trees February through September. Redbreast sunfish are the most abundant game fish in the river. They will hit worms, small grubs or small spinners fished near the shoreline cover. The best fishing is from March through September. Bluegill fishing is limited, but good catches are reported from anglers fishing the same way they would for redbreast.

Thomas, Mills and Boggy creeks: Access is the Nassau Wildlife Management Area west of Yulee. These creeks offer excellent largemouth bass fishing on surface lures and purple, black grape and blue plastic worms fished around submerged trees and stumps. The peak season for trophy bass is January through April. Redbreast sunfish and bluegill fishing is good. Fish with live bait: crickets or worms near underwater trees and stumps. The best fishing is March through September.

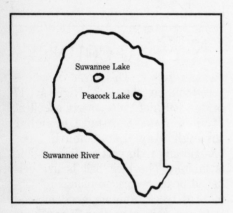

SUWANNEE COUNTY

Suwannee Lake: To get to this 63-acre fish management area go 2 miles east of Live Oak off U.S. Highway 90 and follow the signs. This lake offers excellent largemouth bass fishing on black, purple and motor-oil colored plastic worms when fished around submerged trees and stumps. Although it is a small lake, Suwannee yields 10-pound trophy bass on a regular basis. January through May is peak season. For limit catches of

bluegills and redears use crickets and earthworms fished around submerged trees — and the lake is full of them — from April through September.

Peacock Lake: Six miles east of Live Oak on the south side of U.S. Highway 90, this 148-acre lake offers good largemouth bass fishing. Most of the bass are small, however. Use black or purple worms and fish around the maidencane beds February through May for best results. Bluegill fishing is fair with the majority of the fish taken on live worms or crickets fished near the maidencane beds April through September. Crappie fishing is excellent for anglers drifting live minnows in open water from February through April.

Suwannee River: Good access points are at Suwannee River State Park off U.S. Highway 90 and at Suwannee Springs off S.R. 51. The river offers excellent largemouth bass fishing throughout the year for small yearlings, 2 pounds or less. The best baits are small float-diving lures and purple or black plastic worms fished near the shoreline and around fallen trees or stumps. Redbreast sunfish are the most plentiful game fish in the river and can be caught on small spinners fished near fallen trees and stumps with light tackle. Another good method is a long, limber cane pole baited with crickets and fished along the shoreline as the boat drifts downstream. This is called "throw" or "drop" fishing. Peak season: May through September.

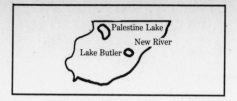

UNION COUNTY

Palestine Lake: One mile west of Lake Butler on County Road 231, this 972-acre lake offers fair bass fishing for yearling largemouths. Use spinnerbaits, black or purple plastic worms and small surface lures. The yearlings can be caught throughout the year. During the winter months, drifting live minnows in open water nets more fish. Jigging with small jigs around brush-type fish attractors is best during summer months. Bluegill and shellcracker fishing is poor. Some fish are taken by fishing worms on the bottom. Sunshine bass fishing is good during the winter months for fishermen drifting minnows in open water.

Lake Butler Lake: This 420-acre lake in the city of Lake Butler is good mostly for schooling bass. Small lures of any type will catch fish, but the most productive is the small plastic worm fished near the maidencane shoreline. The peak season is February through April. Bluegill fishing is poor and the few fish that are caught are taken from the bottom with live worms. Sunshine bass are taken on a regular basis by fishing dead shiners on bottom December through March.

New River: Located 4 miles south of Lake Butler on S.R. 431 at the river bridge, this is a narrow, scenic river with good largemouth fishing in the 1- to 2-pound range. The best lures are small plastic worms and small spinners fished near fallen trees and submerged stumps. Redbreast fishing is excellent on live crickets and small spinners when fished near submerged trees and stumps.

NORTHEAST FLORIDA FISH CAMPS

ALACHUA COUNTY

Orange and Lochloosa lakes

Palmeter's Cross Creek Lodge:
Route 3, Box 124, S.R. 325, Hawthorne, 32640; (904) 466-3228.
Boats, motors, ramp, bait, tackle, gas and oil, guides, lodging, restaurant, groceries, and camping.

Twin Lakes Fish Camp:
Route 3, Box 209, S.R. 325, Hawthorne, 32640; (904) 466-3194.
On Cross Creek, between Lake Orange and Lake Lochloosa
Boats, motors, ramp, bait, tackle, gas and oil, guides, lodging, camp area and canoe rental.

Orange Lake Fish Camp:
P.O. Box 125, Orange Lake, 32681; (904) 591-1870.
On U.S. Highway 441.
Boats, motors, ramp, bait, tackle, gas and oil, lodging, guides, snacks, ice, boat stall rental, RV camping area and canoe rental, restaurant and lounge.

South Shore Fish Camp:
Route 4, Box 820, Citra, 32627; (904) 595-4241.
2 miles west of Citra on S.R. 318.
Boats, motors, ramp, bait, tackle, gas and oil, lodging, guides, snacks and ice.

Finway Fish Camp:
P.O. Box 23, U.S. 301, Hawthorne, 32640; (904) 481-2114.
5 miles south of Hawthorne.
Boats, motors, ramp, bait, tackle, gas and oil, guides, lodging, camp area with hookups, boat and camper storage, and snacks.

Cross Creek Fish Camp:
Route 3, Box 126-A, S.R. 325, Hawthorne, 32640; (904) 466-3424.
Boat, motors, ramp, bait, tackle, gas and oil, guides, lodging, camp area and groceries.

Mike's Fish Camp:
Box 231, McIntosh, 32684; (904) 591-1135.
Off of U.S. Highway 441.
Boats, motors, ramp, bait, tackle, gas and oil, lodging, camp area and snacks.

Griffin's Lodge:
Route 2, Box 2770, S.R. 21, Melrose, 32666; (904) 475-1444.
2.2 miles north of Melrose.
Boats, motors, ramp, bait, guides, cabins.

Santa Fe Lake

Shipman's Camp:
P.O. Box 577, S.R. 1469 West, Earleton, 32631; (904) 468-1568.
Off of S.R. 24.
Boats, motors, bait, tackle, ramp, cabins, camp area and snacks, swimming beach, picnic area, ski area, sailboat area, and marine sales.

Buddy's Landing:
Box 548, S.R. 200-A, Earleton, 32631; (904) 468-2080.
On Lake Santa Fe.
Ramp, gas and oil, cottages, restaurant, wet and dry boat storage.

Newnans Lake

McGilvary's Camp:
7406 S.E. 2nd Ave., Gainesville, 32601; (904) 376-3452.
Off East University Avenue.
Boats, motors, ramps, bait, tackle, gas and oil, cabins, camp area, groceries and ice.

CLAY COUNTY

Doctor's Lake

Whitey's Camp:
S.R. 220, Orange Park, 32073; (904) 264-9198.
3 miles south of Orange Park.
Boats, ramp, bait, tackle, guides, gas and oil, RV camping area, restaurant and ice.

DUVAL COUNTY

Julington Creek

Clark's Camp:
12903 Hood Landing Road, Jacksonville, 32223; (904) 268-3474.
Located on Julington Creek.
Boats, bait, tackle, gas and oil, and a restaurant.

LEVY COUNTY

Withlacoochee River and Lake Rousseau
(Freshwater and Saltwater Access)

Izaak Walton Lodge:
S.R. 40, Box 189, Yankeetown, 32698; (904) 447-2311.
Off of S.R. 40 on 163rd Street.
Lodging and restaurant.

Fin & Feather Camp:
S.R. 40, Star Route 1, Box 700, Morris Avenue, Inglis, 32649; (904) 447-2755.
S.R. 40 between Inglis and Dunnellon
Boat, motors, ramp, tackle, bait, lodging, camping area and snacks.

Suwannee River

Treasure Camp:
S.R. 347, (Fowler's Bluff), Route 1, Box 1076, Chiefland, 32626; (904) 493-2950.
West on U.S. Highway 19-98, 12 miles from Gulf of Mexico on Suwannee River.
Ramp, bait, tackle, gas and oil, lodging, snacks and picnic area, groceries.

Waccasassa River

Waccasassa Marine & Fish Camp:
County Road 326, Gulf Hammock, 32639; (904) 486-2339.
3 miles west of U.S. Highway 19-98
Freshwater and saltwater fishing, ramp, boats (no motors), bait, tackle, gas and oil, guides, motel and efficiencies, campground and snacks.

TAYLOR COUNTY

Steinhatchee River
(Freshwater and Saltwater Access)

Ideal Fish Camp:
P.O. Box 24, Route 51, Steinhatchee, 32359; (904) 498-3877.
On State Road 51.
Boats, motors, lift ramp, dry and wet storage, 10-unit motel, bait, tackle, camp area, gas and oil, ice, guide service.

West Wind Fish Camp:
P.O. Box 240, Steinhatchee, 32359; (904) 498-5254.
On State Road 51.
Boats, bait, gas and oil, motel, tackle shop, RV hookups, boat launch.

Pace's Fish Camp:
P.O. Box 26, Steinhatchee, 32359; (904) 498-3008.
On State Road 51.
Cottages, restaurant (breakfast only), grocery store, tackle, bait, beer, ice, gas and oil, diesel.

Misty Waters Marina:
Riverside Drive, Steinhatchee, 32359; (904) 498-3815
Floating covered dock.

Sportsman's Marina:
600 Riverside Dr., Steinhatchee, 32359; (904) 498-5800.
16-unit motel, bait, tackle, ramp lift, camping, gas and oil, ice, guide service, docking facilities.

Pat Johnson's Fish Camp:
25A Gema Road, Steinhatchee, 32359; (904) 498-3159.
Cabins, camping, charter boat service, ramp.

Suwannee River
(Freshwater and Saltwater Access)

Moore's Marina and Fish Camp:
P.O. Box 178, Suwannee, 32692; (904) 542-7077.
On State Road 349.
Camper hookups, 10-unit motel, bait, tackle, gas and oil, ice, groceries, restaurant, mobile home rental, guide service.

The Tackle Shop:
State Road 349, Suwannee, 32692; (904) 542-7234.
Camp area, dock, gas and oil, tackle, bait, ice, groceries.

NORTHEAST FLORIDA
FISHING
BAROMETER

Month	Largemouth bass	Speckled perch	Sunshine bass	Bream
January	Poor	Fair-good	Excellent	Poor
February	Fair-good	Good-excellent	Excellent	Poor
March	Good-excellent	Excellent	Excellent	Poor-fair
April	Excellent	Good	Good	Fair-good
May	Excellent	Good	Fair	Excellent
June	Good	Fair	Poor	Excellent
July	Fair	Poor	Poor	Good
August	Fair	Poor	Poor	Good
September	Fair-good	Poor	Fair	Good
October	Fair-good	Fair	Good	Fair-good
November	Fair	Fair	Excellent	Fair
December	Poor	Fair-good	Excellent	Poor

8

FISHING IN CENTRAL FLORIDA

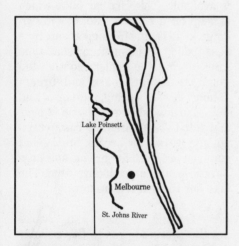

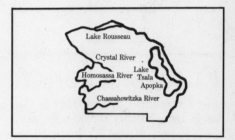

BREVARD COUNTY

Lake Poinsett: This 4,334-acre lake is part of the St. Johns River basin and can be reached off S.R. 520A and S.R. 520 near Rockledge. Bass fishing is fair in the summer but best in the spring and fall. Use plastic worms or live shiners for bait.

CITRUS COUNTY

Lake Tsala Apopka: A series of pools and marshes, this lake extends 22 miles from Floral City northward to Hernando. Its canals connect with the Withlacoochee River. Public ramps are located in Hernando just south of the intersection of U.S. Highway 41 and S.R. 200, off S.R. 44, 1 mile east of Inverness, and off S.R. 48 to Duval Island Road, east of Floral City. It has two fish attractors. Spring and fall are the best times for largemouth bass fishing. Shellcrackers are good in the summer, but the redears hit best in the spring. Sunshine bass hit best during the cooler

se small live shiners or
...nners for sunshine bass.

...e **Rousseau:** This 4,000-acre im-
...undment of the Withlacoochee Riv-
...er lies in Citrus, Levy and Marion
counties and has three public boat
ramps and plenty of fish camps. The
best largemouth bass fishing is during early spring and late fall on live
shiners, plastic worms and crankbaits. Bream hit best in the summer
on crickets and worms. The panfish
also offer decent fishing in the spring
and fall. Watch out for submerged
stumps when fishing this lake.

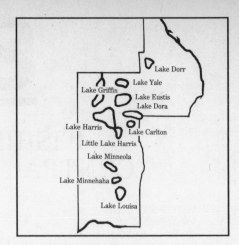

LAKE COUNTY

Lake Carlton: This 382-acre lake is
part of the Oklawaha Chain. The
closest towns are Apopka and Tavares. Lake Carlton is just south of
Lake Dora where a public boat ramp
is available. This circular lake, which
is deep for a Florida lake, was drawn
down in 1977. It offers good sunshine
bass fishing on minnows or shad-type
lures during the cooler months and
good largemouth bass and bream
fishing in the spring, summer and
fall. Use live shiners, plastic worms
and Rat-L-Trap lures for bass; crickets and worms for bream. Spring and
summer are best for bream and bass
but fall is also a productive time. The
lake has three fish attractors.

Lake Dora: Mount Dora and Tavares
are the nearest towns to this popular
4,475-acre lake and both have public
boat ramps. Sunshine bass hit best in
cooler months. Largemouth fishing is
best in the spring and fall on plastic
worms. Bluegill fishing is best in the
summer on crickets and worms.
Shellcrackers hit worms best during
spring and fall.

Lake Dorr: This 1,533-acre lake is
near Altoona. Public access is available at Lake Dorr recreation area
and on the west side of the lake off

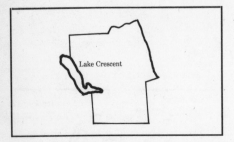

FLAGLER COUNTY

Lake Crescent: Crescent City is the
closest town to this 15,960-acre lake,
which is part of the St. Johns River
basin. Lake Crescent is in Flagler
and Putnam counties and is connected to the St. Johns by Dunn's Creek.
Bass fishing is good in the spring and
fall, and good to fair during the summer on plastic worms and deep-running lures. Specks hit best during the
cooler months on spinners, jigs and
live minnows. Catfishing is good
throughout the year except during
the coldest months. The lake has one
fish attractor.

S.R. 19. Largemouth bass fishing is best during the spring and fall on plastic worms and live shiners.

Lake Eustis: This 7,806-acre lake is part of the Oklawaha Chain and has ramps in Eustis and off U.S. Highway 441 north of Tavares. Sunshine bass hit best in the cooler months on live shiners — small ones are best — spinners and jigs. Largemouth bass fishing on surface lures, plastic worms and larger spinnerbaits is best in the spring and fall.

Lake Griffin: Also part of the Oklawaha Chain, this lake is near Lady Lake and Leesburg and has a public boat ramp in Leesburg on U.S. Highway 441. It has a fish attractor so prolific that it is known as "Bream City." There also are four other attractors. Sunshine bass hit live minnows best in cooler months, but the largemouth fishing is best in the spring and fall on plastic worms, Shad Raps and Rat-L-Traps, as is the shellcracker fishing. Both are fair to good, however, during the summer months. Bluegill fishing is best in the summer on worms and crickets and speck fishing is best in cooler months into early spring.

Lake Harris: This 13,788-acre lake in the Oklawaha Chain is near Leesburg with public ramps off U.S. Highway 27 just south of Leesburg and at the south end of the Howey Bridge on S.R. 19. It offers good speckled perch fishing in late winter and early spring. The best bass fishing for largemouths is in the spring and the top sunshine bass fishing is during the cooler months of the year. Plastic worms and live shiners work best for largemouths. Sunshine bass hit small live shiners best, but they will also take dead shiners used as cut bait when fished on the bottom.

Little Lake Harris: Part of the Oklawaha Chain, this 2,739-acre lake is near Leesburg and has a public ramp off U.S. Highway 19 at the Howey Bridge. Little Lake Harris joins Lake Harris and offers the same type fishing for largemouth bass and sunshine bass.

Lake Louisa: Part of the Clermont Chain, this 3,634-acre lake is near Clermont. Public access is available 4 miles south of Clermont and east of S.R. 561. Lake Louisa has three fish attractors and offers good fishing for schooling largemouth bass from early spring through early summer. Spinnerbaits and live threadfin shad are the best baits for largemouths. Catfishing is good throughout the year except during the coldest months.

Lake Minnehaha: This lake in the Clermont Chain spans 2,261 acres with access from Lake Louisa or Lake Minneola. It has four fish attractors and, except during the cold months, offers good channel catfish angling. The best fishing is for schooling bass in the spring and early summer. Spinnerbaits or small crankbaits are the best lures for the largemouths.

Lake Minneola: This 1,888-acre lake in the Clermont Chain has a public boat ramp in the city of Minneola and contains two fish attractors. Schooling bass fishing is best in spring and early summer on small spinnerbaits and crankbaits. Live shiners also work.

Lake Yale: Part of the Oklawaha Chain, this 4,042-acre lake is near Eustis. There are public boat ramps off state roads 450 and 452 and also at Marsh Memorial Park. Anglers will find good bass fishing year-round, but the best fishing is during the spring and fall. The lake has three fish attractors and offers good speck fishing in late winter and early spring. Sunshine bass fishing is best during the cooler months. Use artificial spoons or live grass shrimp.

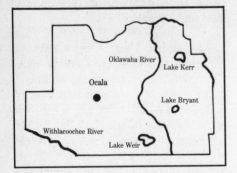

MARION COUNTY

Lake Bryant: Access to this 767-acre lake is off S.R. 40 on Levy Hammock Road. It has two fish attractors. Best bass fishing is in the spring, but largemouths hit well in the fall and summer also. Live shiners catch the most bass and the largest bass. Crappie fishing is good in the spring on live minnows, spinners or jigs such as the Bream Killer or Beetle Spin.

Lake Kerr: The nearest town to this 2,830-acre lake is Salt Springs. A public ramp is off Forest Road 88, south of S.R. 316. Largemouth bass angling is best during the spring with live shiners and plastic worms. Bluegill fishing is best in late spring and summer with live bait such as crickets or earthworms. It has three fish attractors and offers good fly fishing.

Lake Weir: This lake contains 5,685 acres and is near the town of Oklawaha. Public access is available at Hope Beach off Sunset Harbor Road; at Johnson Beach off Alternate 441 in Oklawaha and at Hampton Beach off Alternate 441 south of Oklawaha. The lake has four fish attractors and offers good largemouth

bass fishing in the spring on live shiners or plastic worms. Bluegill angling is best in summer and early fall, but shellcrackers and specks hit best in the spring. Bluegills will take live crickets or earthworms, shellcrackers prefer earthworms and specks prefer small jigs or live minnows.

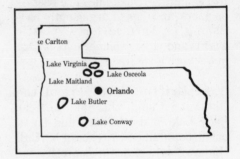

ORANGE COUNTY

Lake Butler: This 1,165-acre lake is part of the Butler Chain or Windermere Chain (both names are used) and is located near Windermere. Public access is available south of S.R. 50 on S.R. 439. However, plans are under way to build a new ramp and picnic area at another site on the chain. Lake Butler is noted for its schooling bass during early spring and early summer. Spinnerbaits and crankbaits are good for schoolers. Lake Butler also is a good lake to wade fish for bass. Fish plastic worms around weedbeds. Its deep holes offer some good speckled perch fishing during the winter and early spring. Other good speck lakes on the chain are Sheen and Pocket. Other good bass fishing lakes include Tibet, Butler, Chase and Sheen.

Lake Conway: Spanning 1,075 acres, the Conway chain is made up of four lakes and is just south of Orlando, near Edgewood. Ramps are at the north end of Randolph Avenue, which intersects with Hoffner Avenue, and on Venetian Drive, which intersects with Hoffner. Bass fishing is good during the summer months but only fair during spring and fall. Plastic worms and live shiners are the best bass producers. This is a good speck fishing lake, especially at night when fishing the deep holes. Use a lantern to attract the fish and bait. Fish with live minnows.

Lake Maitland: This 451-acre lake is part of the Winter Park-Maitland Chain and offers access through Lake Virginia. The city charges a users fee based on the horsepower of the boat motor. Sunshine bass fishing is best during the cooler months. Look for areas with moving water for best results. Bass fishing is good in the spring but only fair in the summer. Speck fishing is best during the cooler months. Use live minnows for bait.

Lake Osceola: Also part of the Winter Park chain, this 157-acre lake offers access through Lake Virginia and a users fee is charged. Excellent sunshine bass fishing can be found here in the cooler months around flowing water. Largemouth bass fishing is good in the spring on plastic worms. Specks hit best during late winter and early spring.

Lake Virginia: Part of the Winter Park Chain, this 223-acre lake is accessible off Fairbanks Avenue near Rollins College in Winter Park. The city charges a users fee according to horsepower of the boat motor. Anglers can find excellent sunshine bass fishing in areas of flowing water. Use small spinners, jigs or live minnows for best results. Largemouth bass fishing is good in the spring and fall on plastic worms. Speckled perch hit best in early spring on live minnows.

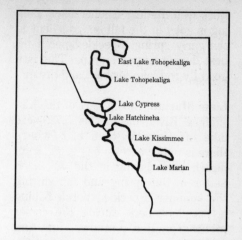

OSCEOLA COUNTY

Lake Cypress: This 4,097-acre lake is part of the Kissimmee River basin and offers public access off County Road 523. It's a good lake for trophy largemouth bass during late spring and summer. Use live shiners, plastic worms or surface lures for best action. The lake also offers good speck fishing during the winter.

Lake Hatchineha: A 6,665-acre lake in the Kissimmee River Chain, it offers access at a fish camp off S.R. 542. This is an excellent lake for fly fishing. There are three fish attractors. Largemouth bass fishing is good in the spring and fall with plastic worms and shiners. Bream fishing is best in spring and summer on artificial flies, live crickets or earthworms for the bream.

Lake Kissimmee: Access to this 34,948-acre lake, which is also part of the Kissimmee Chain, is off Canoe Creek Road, Joe Overstreet Road and at the south end of the lake at U.S. Highway 60. Water fluctuation has produced good to excellent fishing for bass, bluegills, shellcrackers and crappie. Bass fishing is best in early spring; bluegill fishing is best in early spring and summer. Use live shiners for bass. Plastic worms also work well. Redear (shellcracker) fishing is good in the fall but excellent in the early spring. Speckled perch hit best during winter months. This is a good fly rod lake for bass and bream.

Lake Marian: Also a part of the Kissimmee River basin, this 5,739-acre lake off County Road 523 (where there is public access) has good largemouth bass fishing in the fall, even better in the spring and fair during the summer. Speckled perch fishing is excellent here during the cooler months on live minnows, jigs and small spinners.

Lake Tohopekaliga: This 18,810-acre lake — also part of the Kissimmee River basin — has access available on the north end of the lake in Kissimmee and on the south end of the lake at Southport off County Road 531. A public ramp also is at Whaley's Landing off C.R. 525. Water fluctuation on this lake has increased the entire fishery. It offers some of the best trophy bass fishing in the state. Spring and fall are best for bass, but summer can be productive as well. Plastic worms and large shiners are good baits. Live wild shiners will catch even bigger lunkers. Shellcracker fishing is good in the spring on earthworms. Summer is best for bluegills on earthworms or crickets. Speckled perch prefer small live minnows. This lake has six fish attractors and is considered a good lake for wading and fly fishing.

East Lake Tohopekaliga: This 11,968-acre lake has access at East Lake Fish Camp off County Road 530. There are four fish attractors. It is part of the Kissimmee River basin and offers excellent trophy bass fishing in the spring and fall on live shiners, surface lures and plastic worms. Shiners drifted or trolled slowly just off the reedline during early morning

can be a productive method for catching bass. Speckled perch fishing is good during the cooler months. Drift live minnows. Shellcracker fishing is good along the mussel shell bottom in open water. Fish on bottom with live earthworms when you locate the shell bottom.

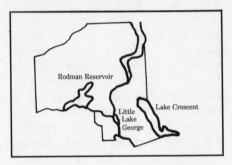

PUTNAM COUNTY

Little Lake George: This 1,416-acre lake is part of the St. Johns River basin. It is accessible from the river. Striped bass fishing is good in the spring and fall on large live shiners. Largemouth bass fishing is good most of the year but best during spring and fall on live shiners, plastic worms and topwater lures. Shellcracker angling is best in the spring on earthworms and bluegill fishing is best in the summer on live worms or crickets.

Rodman Reservoir: Also known as Lake Oklawaha, this is an impoundment of the Oklawaha River. Largemouth bass fishing is good throughout the year but best in the spring on live shiners. Bluegills and shellcrackers hit from early spring through late summer on worms and crickets. Watch for stumps when operating an outboard motor in this area. Anglers have access to this reservoir at Eureka off S.R. 316, Orange Springs, Paynes Landing and near the dam off S.R. 19.

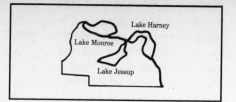

SEMINOLE COUNTY

Lake Harney: Part of the St. Johns River basin, this 6,058-acre lake has access off S.R. 46. Catfishing is good most of the year — coldest months are the exception. Bass fishing is best in the spring on live shiners and plastic worms, but the largemouths also will hit during the fall. Speckled perch fishing is excellent from late winter through early spring on live minnows. Drift fishing is best except when the specks are spawning in shallow water.

Lake Jessup: Access to this 10,011-acre lake is via boat ramp on S.R. 46 or at two fishing camps on the lake: Hiley's or Black Hammock on S.R. 419. Speck fishing is good on live minnows from late winter through early spring. Largemouth bass fishing is best in the spring but also good in the fall. Shellcracker fishing is good from early to late spring on earthworms and bluegill angling is good in the summer and late spring on crickets and worms.

Lake Monroe: Located on the waterfront in Sanford, this large lake is part of the St. Johns River basin. It has two fish attractors and is noted for its good speckled perch fishing during the winter and spring months. Use live minnows and drift fish or fish around the fish attractors — one is on the Enterprise side of the lake and the other is just off the main channel heading south from the Interstate 4 bridge. One access site is on U.S. Highway 17-92, just past the I-4 bridge going north and the other is at Monroe Harbour at the marina. Sunshine bass and largemouth bass hit well in this lake also.

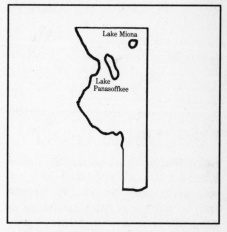

SUMTER COUNTY

Lake Panasoffkee: Public access to this 4,460-acre lake is available on Outlet River off S.R. 470. The best fishing for shellcrackers is in the early spring to early summer. Use redworms and fish on the bottom. Bluegill fishing is only fair in spring and fall, but is good in the summer on crickets or earthworms. Largemouth bass fishing is best in the spring and fall on live shiners and plastic worms, but is only fair in the summer. The lake has two fish attractors.

Lake Miona: Public access to this 418-acre lake is off S.R. 472 near Oxford. Largemouth bass fishing is good in early spring and fall on shiners and plastic worms. Bluegill fishing is good during the summer on earthworms and crickets. Because it is not fished much, Lake Miona offers excellent bass fishing. Use shiners or plastic worms.

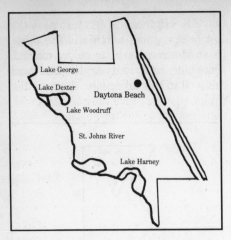

VOLUSIA COUNTY

Lake Dexter: Part of the St. Johns River basin, this 1,902-acre lake is accessible at Astor on S.R. 40. Except for the coldest months, catfishing is good all year. Use earthworms or chicken livers fished on the bottom. Bass fishing for largemouths is best in spring and fall and only fair during the summer. Use live shiners, crankbaits or plastic worms. Bluegill and shellcracker fishing is good from early spring through late summer. Shellcrackers prefer worms, but bluegills will hit worms or crickets. Specks hit best during the cooler months on live minnows or small jigs and spinners.

Lake George: Also part of the St. Johns River basin, this 46,000-acre lake is the largest lake in the system with numerous access points at fishing camps around the lake. A public ramp is at Willow Cover off U.S. Highway 17. Striped bass fishing is good in the spring on large shiners and large plugs such as the Shad Rap. The craters of the old abandoned bombing range area are good fishing spots for stripers. Largemouth bass hit throughout the year but hit best in the spring and second best in the fall. Live shiners, bullhead minnows, plastic worms and topwater lures work best for bass. Crappie

fishing is best during the cooler months on live minnows. Bluegill angling is good in the summer on crickets and earthworms and redear fishing is best in the spring and early summer on live earthworms. The jetties at the mouth of Lake George offer good bass fishing on live shiners and plastic worms.

Lake Woodruff: Another of the St. Johns River basin lakes, Lake Woodruff has 2,200 acres. Access is at Astor on S.R. 40. While catfishing is good all year, it is best during the warmer months. Bluegill fishing is best in the summer with small live baits such as worms, crickets and grass shrimp. Shellcracker angling is best in the spring, but the redear fishing is fair throughout the year, especially during early summer. Use earthworms for bait. Bass fishing for largemouths is good throughout the year on plastic worms and live shiners. The best bass fishing, however, is during the spring months. Speck fishing is best during cooler months. Use live minnows.

CENTRAL FLORIDA'S RIVER SYSTEMS

St. Johns River: This river is unusual because it flows northward through Brevard, Lake, Marion, Orange, Putnam, Seminole, St. Johns and Volusia counties. The St. Johns offers excellent bass fishing from Astor to Sanford's Lake Monroe. Also in these same waters, anglers can find excellent crappie, bluegill, redear and catfish. The same is true for all species from Green Cove Springs to Astor. South of Lake Monroe to Lake Harney is fair fishing. Bass fishing is excellent year-round but best in the spring and fall on live shiners and plastic worms. Catfishing is good throughout the year but best during summer on live earthworms, chicken livers or minnows. Speckled perch fishing is best during the spring on live minnows, small jigs and spinners. Bluegill fishing is best in the summer and redear fishing is best in the spring but good through fall on earthworms. Some scenic areas of the river are in the Lake Woodruff-Dexter area and also from Lake George to Palatka.

Withlacoochee River: This scenic river flows through Sumter, Citrus, Marion and Levy counties. The best fishing is for largemouth bass, bluegills, redear and spotted sunfish from Princess Lake downstream to Dunnellon and from Inglis to Yankeetown. Spotted sunfish hit best in the spring when they are bedding. Use live earthworms or small spinners. Bass fishing is best on live shiners in the spring. Bream fishing is good from early spring through early fall on earthworms.

Oklawaha River: Flowing through Lake, Marion and Putnam counties, this river offers excellent bass fishing all year, especially during the spring. Live shiners work best. Bream fishing is good throughout the year but best during spring and summer when they are bedding. Use small spinnerbaits or live earthworms for best bream catches. The best area is from the north end of Lake Griffin to where it intersects the St. Johns River. Scenic areas include an area from the S.R. 40 bridge to where it meets the St. Johns River.

Crystal River: Located in Citrus County, this is a picturesque, springfed river that flows westward to the Gulf of Mexico. It offers fair bass, bluegill and shellcracker fishing throughout the year. Crankbaits and spinnerbaits work best for bass; earthworms are best for bream. Mangrove snapper, redfish, sea trout and other saltwater species also frequent these waters, especially during the colder months. Live shrimp are good baits for the saltwater species.

Chassahowitzka River: Located in Citrus County, this shallow, springfed river flows into the Gulf of Mexico. Bass, bluegill and redear fishing is good throughout the year, but it is best during spring and fall. Use live shiners, plastic worms or crankbaits for best results. For saltwater species, which are also available in this river, use live shrimp.

Homosassa River: This scenic river flows from Nature's Giant Fishbowl, an area attraction, westward to the Gulf of Mexico. While fishing is good year-round for bass and bream, it is best during the spring and fall. Use plastic worms, shiners or spinnerbaits for bass. Earthworms and small spinnerbaits are good for bream. This is an excellent river for mangrove snapper. The fish are scrappy and delectable. Look for bends in the river with fallen or overhanging trees, anchor your boat and fish on the bottom with a No. 3 hook with a split shot, and live shrimp. The Crow's Nest, located where the Gulf and the river meet, is a favorite restaurant of mine after a morning of fishing. Accessible only by boat, it specializes in fresh seafood. Shell Island, across the river from the restaurant, is a good place to beach your boat, kick off your shoes and relax.

CENTRAL FLORIDA
FISH CAMPS

BREVARD COUNTY

Lake Poinsett

Lake Poinsett Lodge:
S.R. 520-A and Lake Poinsett, Cocoa; 5665 Lake Poinsett Road, Cocoa 32926-2304; (305) 636-0045.
Restaurant, private ramp, boats, motors, bait, groceries.

Lake Washington

Lake Washington Resort:
6000 Lake Washington Road, Melbourne, 32935; (305) 254-9932.
Private ramp, bait, ice, living units, and boat storage.

St. Johns River

Camp Holly:
St. Johns River and U.S. Highway 192 West; Star Route Box 1135, Melbourne, 32901; (305) 723-2179.
Private ramp, boats, motors, oil, tackle, bait, ice, living units and groceries. Airboat rides.

Lone Cabbage Fish Camp:
S.R. 520 West, Cocoa, 32922; (305) 632-4199.
Boats, bait, canoes, airboat rides, ice, beer, wine, restaurant and guide service.

CITRUS COUNTY

Chassahowitzka River

Chassahowitzka River Lodge:
8501 W. Miss Maggie Drive, Homosassa, 32464; (904) 382-2081.
Ramp, boats, bait, ice, restaurant, travel trailer spaces, living units.

Lykes Chassahowitzka River Campground:
Off U.S. Highway 19 and S.R. 480; P.O. Box 890, Homosassa Springs, 32647; (904) 382-2200.
Ramp, boats, bait, tackle shop, groceries, licenses, and campground.

Crystal River

Knox Bait House:
558 N.W. 3rd Ave., Crystal River, 32629; (904) 795-2771.
Ramp, bait, tackle shop, ice, groceries, gas and oil, guide service. Wet and dry storage, complete marine service.

Brown's Bluecrab:
268 N.W. 3rd St., Crystal River 32629; (904) 795-2932 or (904) 795-4233.
Ramp, bait, ice, gas and oil.

Plantation Inn Marina:
A quarter mile west of U.S. Highway 19; P.O. Box 1093, Crystal River, 32629; (904) 795-5797.
Ramp, boats with motors, guides, pool, ice, scuba rentals, living units, canoes, and paddle boats.

Floral City Lake

Moonrise Resort:
U.S. Highway 41; 8801 E. Moonrise Lane, Box 18, Floral City, 32636; (904) 726-2553.
Ramp, boats, beverages, living units and RV sites, mobile home lots.

Halls River

Nature's Marina
S.R. 490A West and Hall River; P.O. Box 1326, Homosassa Springs, 32647; (904) 628-4344 (marina) or (904) 628-2892 (campground).
Private ramp, boats, travel trailer spaces, bait, tackle shop, ice, groceries, full marina, convention hall, and motors.

Hernando Lake

Hernando Fishing Lodge:
U.S. Highway 41 and S.R. 200; Star Route 2, Box 99, Hernando, 32642; (904) 726-8403.
Boats and living units.

Watson's Camp:
Off U.S. Highway 41; P.O. Box 126, Inverness, 32651; (904) 726-2225.
Ramp and living units.

Homosassa River

Ward's Resort:
S.R. 490-A; P.O. Box 268, Homosassa Springs, 32647; (904) 628-2551.
Ramp, boats, motors, guides, bait, tackle shop, efficiencies, and boat slips.

Macrae Bait House:
Homosassa Inn; Box 318, Homosassa, 32646; (904) 628-2922.
Ramp, boats, motors, ice, gas, bait, free maps, living units, motel units and guides (salt and freshwater).

Riverside Inn:
West of U.S. Highway 19; P.O. Box 258, Homosassa, 32646; (904) 628-2474.
Ramp, boats, motors, bait, tackle, ice, guide service, travel trailer spaces, gas and oil, and living units.

Lake Rousseau

Lake Rousseau Safari Campground:
10811 N. Coveview Terrace, Crystal River, 32629; (904) 795-6336.
Ramp, boats, travel trailer spaces, full hookups, 6 rental units, guide service, bait, tackle, ice and groceries.

Lake Tsala Apopka

Cypress Lodge:
1025 S.R. 44 East, Inverness, 32650; (904) 726-1272.
Ramp, boats, motors, guide service, ice, swimming area, bait, tackle, gas and oil, and lakefront efficiencies.

Withlacoochee River

Trails End Camp:
12900 E. Trails End Road, Floral City, 32636; (904) 726-3699.
Ramp, boats, motors, bait, tackle shop, ice, camping facilities with and without hookups, gas, living units, licenses, beer and snacks.

Turner Camp:
3033 N. Hooty Point, Inverness, 32650; (904) 726-2685.
Ramp, boats, motors, bait, tackle, ice, groceries, travel trailer spaces, camping and living units.

FLAGLER COUNTY

Dead Lake

Flagler Fish Camp:
St. Johns Park; Route 1, Box 174, Bunnell, 32010; (904) 437-3451.
Ramp, boats, motors, bait, ice, living units, cabins, camping, tackle.

Flagler Beach Marina and Boat Works:
S.R. A1A; P.O. Box 1864, Flagler Beach, 32036; (904) 439-2616.
Service, ice, showers, lifts for boats, wet and dry storage, laundry.

LAKE COUNTY

Clermont Chain of Lakes

Lake Susan Lodge and Marina:
South Lakeshore Drive; Route 3, Box 141, Clermont, 32711; (904) 394-3964.
Ramp, boats, motors, pool, bait, tackle shop, ice, gas, beverages, rental stalls, living units and restaurant.

Dead River

Palm Garden Fishing Camp:
U.S. Highway 441; Box 547, Tavares, 32778; (904) 343-2024.
Ramp, boats, bait, tackle shop, ice, beverages, gas, sandwiches, shower, laundry and living units.

Lake Dora

Mount Dora Marina:
148 Charles Street, Mount Dora, 32757; (904) 383-3150.
Bait, tackle shop, ice, beverages, gas, marine hardware, boat and engine repair, slip rentals, boat, motor and trailer sales.

Lake George

Silver Glen Springs Campground:
West shore of Lake George; Route 2, Box 3000, Fort McCoy, 32637; (904) 685-2514.
Ramp, bait, ice, guides (upon request), snacks, and canoes.

Lake Griffin

Al Jana Fish Camp:
3100 U.S. Highway 441, Leesburg, 32748; (904) 787-2429.
Ramp, boats, beverages, living units, travel trailer spaces, bait and tackle.

Jack's Cottages:
Off U.S. Highway 27 on Eagles Nest Road; Route 2, Box 2050, Fruitland Park, 32731; (904) 728-4458.

Ramp, boats, and living units (year-round tenants preferred).

Big Cypress Cottages:
U.S. Highway 441; Route 6, Box 1120, Leesburg, 32748; (904) 787-1282.

Boats, motors, swimming beach and pool, living units.

Lake Griffin Resort:
Off U.S. Highway 27 on Griffinview Drive; Route 2, Box 777, Lady Lake, 32659; (904) 753-3241.

Ramp, boats, motors, bait, tackle shop, gas, beverages, swimming pool, laundry and living units.

Lazy Oak Resort:
2601 North Griffin Drive, Leesburg, 32748; (904) 787-3626.

Ramp, boats, motors, bait, tackle shop, beverages, freezer available, gas and living units.

Morgan's Fish Camp:
S.R. 466-A; Route 3, Box 1800, Fruitland Park, 32731; (904) 787-4916.

Ramp, boats, motors, bait, tackle shop, ice, groceries, gas, travel trailer and hookups, living units.

Pine Island Fish Camp:
Lake Griffin Road; Route 2, Box 630, Lady Lake, 32659; (904) 753-2972.

Ramp, boats, bait, tackle shop, ice, gas, travel trailer hookups, boat stalls, showers and laundry.

Shady Acres Fishing Resort:
S.R. 44; Route 5, Box 137, Leesburg, 32788; (904) 787-5988.

Ramp, boats, motors, bait, tackle shop, beverages, gas and living units.

Twin Palms Resort and Marina:
S.R. 466-A; Route 3, Box 1500, Fruitland Park, 32748; (904) 787-4514.

Ramp, bait, tackle shop, gas, boat stalls for rent and living units.

Fisherman's Wharf:
Eagle Nest Road; Route 2, Box 2060, Fruitland Park, 32731; (904) 787-4240.

Boat slips only. Mobile-home lots.

Haines Creek

Bay Island Cottages:
Oklawaha Drive, Bassville Park; Route 4, Box 803, Leesburg, 32748; (904) 742-2634.

Ramp, boats, bait, tackle shop, beverages, snacks, gas, 1 travel trailer hookup, living units.

Black Bass Fishing Resort:
S.R. 44 at Haines Creek Bridge; Route 14, Box 216, Leesburg, 32788; (904) 728-1005.

Ramp, boats, guide, bait, ice, groceries, living units.

Sparky's Fish Camp:
Oklawaha Drive, Bassville Park; Route 4, Box 823, Leesburg, 32788; (904) 742-1216.

Ramp, boats, cane poles, electrical hookups, bait, beverages, showers and living units.

Spillway Park:
Haines Creek Bridge at Lisbon; Route 14, Box 217, Leesburg, 32788; (904) 728-3420.

Beverages, snacks, dock fishing, RV spaces and boat slips.

Winton's Marina:
S.R. 44 at Haines Creek Bridge; Route 14, Box 215, Leesburg, 32748; (904) 787-6306.

Ramp, bait, ice, beverages, gas, boat slip for rent.

Fisherman Cove:
U.S. Highway 19; Box 1205-C, Route 1, Tavares, 32778; (904) 343-1233.

Ramp, boats, motors, gas, RV spaces, beverages, laundry, showers, recreational building, living units.

Florida Anglers Resort:
6975 U.S. Highway 441 South, Leesburg, 32748; (904) 343-4141.

Ramp, boats, motors, swimming beach, shuffleboard, playground, barbecue grills, laundry and living units.

Kleiser's Fish Camp:
Lane Park Road, off U.S. Highway 19; Route 1, Box 1170, Tavares, 32778; (904) 343-3454.

Ramp, boats, motors, bait, tackle shop, ice, beverages, snacks, gas.

Lake Louisa

Lake Louisa State Park:
Lake Nellie Road; Route 1, Box 107, Clermont, 32711; (904) 394-2280.

No boat ramp. Opens 8 a.m.; closes at sundown. Picnic area, swimming, showers, restrooms.

Lake Minnehaha

Cypress Cove Resort:
S.R. 561; Route 3, Box 21, Clermont, 32711; (904) 394-2880.

Ramp, beverages, gas, travel trailer hookups, wet and dry boat storage, mobile-home park and living units.

St. Johns River

Allen's Cottages:
Old S.R. 40; Route 2, Box 113, Astor, 32002; (904) 759-2130.
Boats, motors, bait, ice, groceries, and living units.

Powell's Campground:
Alco Road; Route 1, Box 17, Astor, 32002; (904) 759-2010.
Ramp, bait, ice, guides, groceries, gas, tackle, laundry and showers.

Astor/St. Johns Marine:
Old S.R. 40; P.O. Box 214, Astor, 32002; (904) 759-2172.
Ramp, ice, fuel and service.

MARION COUNTY

Bowers Lake

Tall Pines Park Bait and Tackle:
Route 3, Box 60, Oklawaha, 32679; (904) 288-4211.
Ramp, living units, boat rentals, boat slips, bait, tackle, ice, oil and L.P. gas.

Lake Bryant

Lake Bryant Camp:
Levy Hammock Road, south of S.R. 40; Route 1, Box 950, Oklawaha, 32679; (904) 625-2376.
Ramp, boats, motors, bait, tackle shop, ice, beverages, groceries, licenses, camping area, swimming, skiing, living units, L.P. gas, oil, and cable TV.

Lake Jumper

Lake Jumper Fish Camp:
3171 N.E. County Road 314-A, Silver Springs, 32688; (904) 625-2345.
Ramp, boats.

Lake Kerr

Lake Kerr Park:
Route 3, Box 735, Fort McCoy, 32637; (904) 685-2557.
Ramp, boats, motors, living units and swimming area.

Little Lake Kerr

Anchor Inn Cottages:
Route 3, Box 1240, Fort McCoy, 32637; (904) 685-2330.
Ramp, boats, motors, bait, living units, picnicking and camping.

Mill Dam Pond

Half Moon Camp:
S.R. 40; Route 3, Box 610, Silver Springs, 32688; (904) 625-2276.
Ramp, tackle shop, ice, groceries, camping.

Oklawaha River

Nelson's Fish Camp:
S.R. 42; Route 1, Box 1366-94, Umatilla, 32784; (904) 821-2421.
Ramp, boats, motors, guides, bait, tackle shop, ice, groceries, oil and living units.

Fisherman's Cove:
S.R. 42; Route 1, Box 1085, Weirsdale, 32695; (904) 821-3701.
Ramp, boats, motors, guides, bait, tackle shop, ice, groceries, oil and living units.

Orange Lake

Citra Fish Camp:
S.R. 318; Route 4, Box 990, Citra, 32627; (904) 595-3061.
Ramp, bait, tackle shop, ice, groceries.

Heagy's Fish Camp:
U.S. Highway 441; P.O. Box 344, Orange Lake, 32681; (904) 591-1966.
Boats, motors, guides, bait, tackle shop, ice, groceries, 2 cottages, R.V. parking.

McIntosh Fish Camp:
U.S. Highway 441 and Avenue H; P.O. Box 135, McIntosh, 32664; (904) 591-1302.
Ramp, boats, motors, pool, bait, tackle shop, ice, gas and oil, boat stall rentals, service available, living units, RV spaces, laundry.

Mike's Fish Camp:
U.S. Highway 441; P.O. Box 231, McIntosh, 32664; (904) 591-1135.
Ramp, boats, motors, bait, tackle shop, groceries and living units.

Orange Lake Fish Camp:
U.S. Highway 441; Box 125, Orange Lake, 32681; (904) 591-1870.
Ramp, boats, motors, guides, bait, tackle shop, ice, private boat storage sheds and living units.

South Shore Fish Camp:
S.R. 318; Route 4, Box 820, Citra, 32627; (904) 595-4241.
Ramp, boats, motors, bait, tackle shop, ice, beverages, gas and oil, living units.

Salt Springs Run

Carroll's Waterfront:
Salt Springs; Route 2, Box 2060, Fort McCoy, 32637; (904) 685-2185.
Ramp, boats, bait, ice and camping.

Silver Glen Springs

Silver Glen Springs:
U.S. Highway 19; Route 2, Box 3000, Fort McCoy, 32637; (904) 685-2514.
Ramp, guides (fishing and hunting), ice, living units, marina (up to 60-foot boats), snacks.

Lake Waldena

Lake Waldena Resort:
S.R. 40; Route 4, Box 300, Silver Springs, 32688; (904) 625-2851.
Boats, canoes, ice, groceries, swimming, camping, picnicking.

Lake Weir

Sunset Harbor Grocery:
10333 S.E. Sunset Harbor Road, Summerfield, 32691; (904) 288-3315.
Tackle shop, ice, groceries, dock, sandwich and sub shop, ice cream parlor.

Withlacoochee River

Anglers Resort and Motel:
U.S. Highway 41; P.O. Box 515, Dunnellon, 32630; (904) 489-2397.
Boats, motors, guides, bait, tackle shop, beverages, gas and oil, licenses, and living units.

Fish-n-Fun Lodge:
302 Palmetto Way, Dunnellon, 32630; (904) 489-2697.
Boats, motors, living units, guides, bait, tackle shop, ice, gas and oil.

ORANGE COUNTY

Lake Ivanhoe

Boat ramp and dock.
Orlando: North Orange Avenue and Ivanhoe Terrace.

Lake Underhill

Boat ramp and dock.
Orlando: Lake Underhill Drive and Conway Road.

Lake Fairview

Boat ramp, dock, swimming beach.
Orlando: Lee Road and U.S. Highway 441.

Clear Lake

Boat ramp.
Orlando: Off Gore Street, near Tampa Avenue and Orange Center Boulevard.

Lake Apopka

Boat ramp and dock. Not recommended for boats longer than 18 feet.
Near Apopka, off S.R. 437 at Magnolia Park.

Lake Beauclair

Boat ramp, picnicking and camping facilities.
Tangerine: At Trimble Park off U.S. Highway 441 North.

Lake Conway

Boat ramp.
Orlando: Randolph Avenue in Pine Castle.

Boat ramp. For boats less than 12 feet.
Orlando: Ferncreek Avenue in Pine Castle.

Lake Jessamine

Boat ramp.
Orlando: Bywater Drive.

Boat ramp. For boats less than 12 feet.
Orlando: Woodsmere Avenue, just off South Orange Blossom Trail, between Holden Avenue and Oak Ridge Road.

Lake Down

Boat ramp. For boats up to 16 feet.
Windermere: Conroy Road, a half mile east of Apopka-Vineland Road.

Lake Mary Jane

Boat ramp, picnicking.
South of Orlando at Moss Park: Off S.R. 15 on Moss Park Road between Lake Mary Jane and Lake Hart.

Lake Maitland
(Winter Park and Maitland Chain)

Boat ramp. Check with Winter Park Police Department for special regulations.
Maitland: At Live Oak Street.

Lake Virginia
(Winter Park and Maitland Chain)

Boat ramp. Check with Winter Park Police Department for special regulations.
Winter Park: At Dinky Dock, on Ollie Street near Rollins College.

OSCEOLA COUNTY

Lake Marian

Lake Marian Marina:
County Road 523; Star Route, Box 615, Kenansville, 32739; (305) 436-1021.
Ramp, boats, motors, bait, ice, guides, living units, poles, camping, tackle, gas and oil.

Shingle Creek (West Lake)

Harbor Oaks Marina:
3605 Marsh Road, Kissimmee, 32741; (305) 846-1321.
Ramp, canoes, bait, ice, campsites, tackle, snacks.

East Lake Tohopekaliga

East Lake Fish Camp:
3680 E. Boggy Creek Road, Kissimmee, 32741; (305) 348-2040.
Ramp, boats, motors, bait, ice, groceries, 1 living unit, RV park.

West Lake Tohopekaliga

Big Toho Marina:
101 Lakeshore Blvd., Kissimmee, 32741; (305) 846-2124.
Ramp, boats, motors, bait, ice, guides, groceries, snack bar, tackle, reel repair.

Richardson's Fish Camp:
1550 Scotty's Road, Kissimmee, 32741; (305) 846-6540.
Ramp, boats, motors, bait, ice, guides, groceries, living units and restaurant.

Red's Fish Camp:
6050 Seaman Ave., St. Cloud, 32769; (305) 892-8795.
Ramp, boats, motors, bait, ice, guides, groceries, campsites.

Scotty's Fish Camp:
1554 Scotty's Road, Kissimmee, 32743; (305) 847-3840.
Ramp, boats, motors, bait, ice, guides, groceries, living units and campsites.

Southport Park:
2001 Southport Road, Kissimmee, 32741; (305) 933-5822.
Ramp, boats, motors, bait, ice, guides, groceries, 53 campsites, tackle, fish cleaning station, shower room, playground area and picnic pavilions.

POLK COUNTY

Lake Kissimmee

Camp Lester:
14400 Reese Drive, Lake Wales, 33853; (813) 696-1123.
Guides, licenses, tackle, bait, camping facilities, rental cabins, swimming pool, ice, ramp.

Grape Hammock:
1400 Grape Hammock Road, Lake Wales, 33853; (813) 692-1500.
Boats, bait, guides, camping facilities, ramp, cottages.

Outdoor Resort River Ranch:
On Kissimmee River; U.S. Highway 60 East, Lake Wales, 33853; (813) 692-1321.
Bait, tackle, boats, motors, licenses, guides, motel, RV, tenting, cottages, efficiencies, grocery store.

Shady Oaks:
Off U.S. Highway 60; 1800 Shady Oaks Road, Lake Wales, 33853; (813) 692-1261.
Tackle, bait, snack bar, ramp, groceries, RV hookups, gas and oil, rental cabins.

The Oasis:
25601 U.S. Highway 60 East, Lake Wales, 33853; (813) 692-1594.
Boats, living units, guides, licenses, tackle, bait, groceries, camping facilities, ramp, self-contained trailers, RV hookups, gas.

Public Landing:
U.S. Highway 60, east of Lake Wales, at Kissimmee River Bridge above dam entrance.

PUTNAM COUNTY

Dunns Creek

Dunns Creek Fishing Resort:
U.S. Highway 17 and Dunns Creek; Star Route 3, Box 1497, Satsuma, 32089; (904) 325-7772.
Ramp and 2 overnight hookups.

Georgia Boy Fishing Village:
U.S. Highway 17 and Dunns Creek; Star Route 2, Box 17, Satsuma, 32089; (904) 325-7764.
Ramp, bait, ice, guides and living units.

Crescent Lake

Lake Crescent Resort:
U.S. Highway 17 north; 904 N. Summitt, Crescent City, 32012; (904) 698-2485.
Boat, motor, guides, living units and RV sites.

Tangerine Cove:
U.S. Highway 17 north; Route 1, Box 10, Crescent City, 32012; (904) 698-1170.
Ramp, boats, motors, bait, RVs, gas, ice, guides, groceries, living units and restaurant.

Lake George and St. Johns River

Camp Henry:
On County Road 309; Star Route 522, Georgetown, 32039; (904) 467-2282.
Ramp, boats, motors, bait, ice, guides, living units, RV spaces, snack shop, tackle and motor repair.

Lunker Lodge:
P.O. Box 386, Georgetown, 32039; (904) 467-2240.
Ramp, bait, ice, guides, living units, restaurant, covered boat stalls.

Merck's Landing:
P.O. Box 7, Georgetown, 32039; (904) 467-2310.
Ramp, boats, motors, bait, ice, guides, living units, oyster bar and restaurant, RV sites.

Trophy Bass Lodge:
Box 514, Star Route, Georgetown, 32039; (904) 467-2002.
Ramp, boats, motors, bait, guides, living units, RV sites, pool.

St. Johns Harbor

Shell Harbor:
P.O. Box 619, Satsuma, 32089; (904) 467-2330.
Ramp, ice, guides, living units, restaurant, boat rental, swimming.

St. Johns River

Angler's Paradise:
Star Route 2, Box 107, Crescent City, 32012; (904) 467-2000.
Boats, motors, bait, ice, guides, living units, restaurant, and swimming pool.

Bass Haven Lodge:
P.O. Box 147, Welaka, 32093; (904) 467-2392.
Boats, motors, bait, guides, lodge rooms, motel and private dining.

Bass World:
P.O. Box 430, Georgetown, 32039; (904) 467-2267.
Ramp, boats, motors, bait, ice, guides and living units.

Wolfe's Fish Camp:
P.O. Box 118, Welaka, 32093; (904) 467-2770.
Boats, motors, living units and RV parking.

Gateway Fishing Camp:
Star Route 1, Box 350, Crescent City, 32012; (904) 467-2411.
Ramp, boats, motors, bait, ice, guides, living units and RV hookups.

Huber's Fish Camp:
Star Route 1, Box 266, Crescent City, 32012; (904) 467-2288.
Ramp, boats, RV sites.

Norton's Place:
P.O. Box 458, Welaka, 32093; (904) 467-2464.
Boats, motors, bait, ice, guides, groceries, living units.

Sunset Landing:
P.O. Box 332, Welaka, 32093; (904) 467-2166.
Ramp, boats, motors, bait, guides, living units.

Trail Boss:
P.O. Box 1140, Welaka, 32093; (904) 467-2319.
Ramp, boats, motor, living units, bait, campsites.

ST. JOHNS COUNTY

Trout Creek

Pacetti's Marina and Fish Camp:
Box 366, Orangedale Route, Green Cove Springs, 32043; (904) 284-5356 or (904) 264-1102.
Ramp, boats, motors, bait, ice, guides, groceries, living units, RV sites, restaurant and laundry.

St. Johns River (saltwater)

Riverside Fish Camp:
305 Valina Road, St. Augustine, 32084; (904) 829-8314.
Boats, motors, bait, fish sales, dock.

Pellicer Creek Campgrounds:
Route 4, Box 209E, St. Augustine, 32084;
(904) 794-9905.
Boats, bait, ice and groceries.

SEMINOLE COUNTY

Lake Jessup

Hiley's Fish Camp:
Lake Jessup off S.R. 419; P.O. Box 841,
Oviedo, 32765; (305) 365-3831.
Ramp, boats, motors, bait, ice, groceries and
boat storage.

Wekiva River

Katie's Wekiva River Landing:
190 Katie's Cove, Wekiva Park Drive, Sanford, 32771; (305) 322-4470.
Ramp, boats, motors, bait, ice, groceries, 1
living unit, RV hookups, canoes.

Wekiva Marina:
1002 Miami Springs Drive, Longwood,
32750; (305) 862-1500.
Ramp, bait, ice, groceries, restaurant, rental
canoes.

Wekiva River Haven:
9 miles west of Sanford on S.R. 46; 160 Haven Trail, Sanford, 32771; (305) 322-1909.
Ramp, boats, motors, bait, ice, groceries.

Osteen Bridge Fish Camp:
St. Johns River and S.R. 415; Route 2, Box
43, Sanford, 32771; (305) 322-3825.
Ramp, boats, motors, bait, ice, guides, guns
and ammunition.

Lindsay's Fish Camp:
5 miles east of Geneva on S.R. 46; P.O. Box
341, Geneva, 32732; (305) 349-5121.
Boats, bait, beverages, snacks, overnight
camping and RV hookups.

Marina Isle:
3812 W. State Road 46, Oviedo, 32765;
(305) 322-4786.
Boats, motors, bait, tackle, ice, gas, ramp
and campground.

SUMTER COUNTY

Lake Panasoffkee

Basswater Lodge:
S.R. 470; Route 1, Box 91, Lake Panasoffkee, 33538; (904) 793-3972.
Ramp, swimming, beverages and camping
hookups.

Henry's Marina:
S.R. 470; P.O. Box 129, Lake Panasoffkee,
33538; (904) 793-2624.
Ramp, boats, motors, guides, bait, tackle
shop, snacks, tavern, restaurant.

Pana Vista Lodge:
S.R. 470; Pana Vista Lodge, Lake Panasoffkee, 33538; (904) 793-2061.
Ramp, boats, motors, guides, bait, tackle
shop, ice, living units, 30 camping units, and
repair service.

Ri-La-Ca Marina and Campgrounds:
I-75 and S.R. 470; Box 1555, Lake Panasoffkee, 33538; (904) 793-6339.
Ramp, boats, motors, tackle shop, bait, ice,
beverages, campsites, living units, and RV
park.

Turtleback Camp:
S.R. 470; Route 1, Box 102, Lake Panasoffkee, 33538; (904) 793-2051.
Ramp, boats, motors, boat mooring, bait,
tackle shop, ice, beverages, RV and campsites,
living units, cottage rentals.

Withlacoochee River

Wynn Haven Camp:
S.R. 48; Route 2, Box 636, Bushnell, 33513;
(904) 793-4744.
Ramp, boats, motors, campsites, gas and 1
living unit.

VOLUSIA COUNTY

Highland Park Run

Highland Park Fish Camp:
2640 W. Highland Park Road, DeLand,
32720; (904) 734-2334.
Ramp, boats, motors, bait, ice, guides, groceries, 1 living unit, boat stalls, dry storage
with marine forklift, tackle, and 50-unit campground.

Lake Beresford

Tropical Apartments and Marina:
1485 Lakeview Drive, DeLand, 32720;
(904) 734-3080.
Ramp, boats, motors, bait, ice, living units
and pool.

Daisy Lake

North Shell Fish Camp:
2981 North Shell Road, DeLand, 32720;
(904) 736-2286.
Ramp, boats, bait, ice, 1 living unit.

Lake George

Pine Island Fish Camp:
1600 Lake George Road, Seville, 32090; (904) 749-2818.
Ramp, boats with motors, bait, ice, guides, groceries and campground, boat rentals.

Spring Garden Lake

Tedder's Fish Camp:
1 mile north of U.S. Highway 17 on DeLeon Springs Boulevard; Box 852, DeLeon Springs, 32028; (904) 985-9365.
Ramp, boats, motors, and bait.

St. Johns River

Hall's Lodge:
East end of Astor bridge; Route 2, Box 119, Astor, 32002; (904) 749-2505.
Ramp, boats, ice, bait, gas and motel.

Highbanks Marina and Camp Resort:
End of Highbanks Road at St. Johns River; Post Office 276, DeBary; (305) 668-4491.
Ramp, bait, ice, groceries, 1 living unit, campground, and RV hookups.

Sunshine Line:
Marker 51 on the St. Johns; Box 3558, De-Land, 32720; (904) 736-9422.
Ramp, ice, houseboat rentals.

Hontoon Marina:
2317 River Ridge Road, DeLand, 32720; (904) 734-2007.
Ramp, boats, motors, bait, ice, guides, groceries and living units.

Jungle Den:
1½ miles north of S.R. 40; 1820 Jungle Den Road, Astor, 32002; (904) 749-2264.
Ramp, boats, motors, bait, ice, guides, 44 living units, restaurant, general store, motel and efficiency apartments.

Lemon Bluff Fish Camp:
Off S.R. 415; Lemon Bluff Road, Osteen, 32764; (305) 322-6843.
Ramp, bait, ice, guides, groceries, restaurant, gas and camper sites.

Parramore's Fish Camp:
Route 2, Box 156, Astor, 32002; (904) 749-2721.
Ramp, boats, motors, bait, ice, guides, living units, RV parking and hookups, swimming pool, bathhouse.

Shady Oak Fish Camp:
2984 Old New York Avenue, DeLand, 32720; (904) 734-9715.
Bait and ice.

South Moon Camp:
1977 South Moon Road, Astor, 32002; (904) 749-2383.
Ramp, boats, motors, ice, bait, living units, gas, tackle shop.

Volusia Bar Fish Camp:
7 miles off U.S. Highway 17 west; Route 1, Box 93, Pierson, 32080; (904) 749-2715.
Ramp, boats, motors, bait, ice, groceries, living units.

CENTRAL FLORIDA FISHING BAROMETER

Month	Largemouth bass	Speckled Perch	Sunshine Bass	Bream
January	Fair	Excellent	Fair	Poor
February	Excellent	Excellent	Excellent	Poor
March	Excellent	Good	Good	Poor
April	Good	Fair	Fair	Good
May	Good	Poor	Poor	Good
June	Good	Poor	Poor	Excellent
July	Fair	Poor	Poor	Excellent
August	Fair	Poor	Poor	Excellent
September	Fair	Poor	Poor	Poor
October	Good	Fair	Fair	Poor
November	Fair	Good	Good	Poor
December	Fair	Excellent	Excellent	Poor

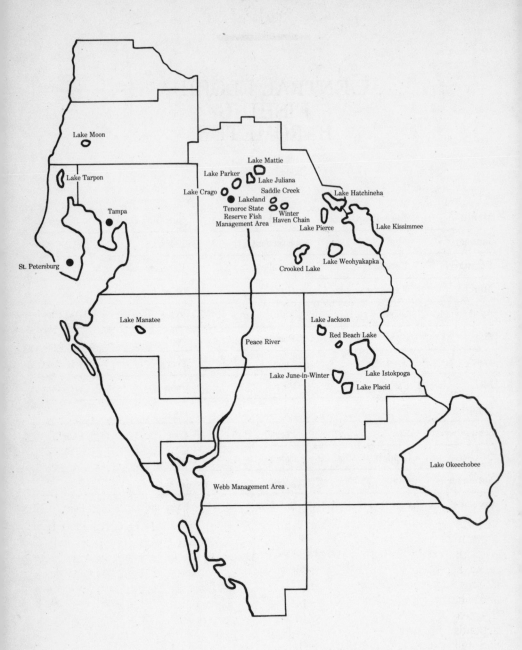

Lake Moon

Lake Tarpon

Tampa

St. Petersburg

Lake Parker
Lake Crago
Lakeland
Tenoroc State
Reserve Fish
Management Area

Lake Mattie
Lake Juliana
Saddle Creek
Winter
Haven Chain

Lake Hatchineha

Lake Kissimmee

Lake Pierce

Crooked Lake

Lake Weohyakapka

Lake Manatee

Peace River

Lake Jackson
Red Beach Lake

Lake June-in-Winter

Lake Istokpoga
Lake Placid

Webb Management Area

Lake Okeechobee

9

FISHING IN
SOUTH FLORIDA

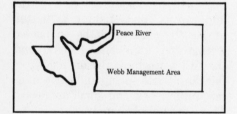

Peace River

Webb Management Area

CHARLOTTE
COUNTY

Peace River: This scenic river, which flows from Polk to Charlotte County, is popular for canoe fishing, but sometimes even a canoeist must portage the canoe during dry weather. Near Arcadia, the river offers good fishing for largemouth bass, bluegills and shellcrackers. Even more than the season of the year, bass fishing depends on water level. Early spring and fall are usually the best times. Fish the deep holes of the river with plastic worms or spinnerbaits. Bream fishermen find good fishing in the deep holes, around tree stumps and fallen treetops during spring, sum-

mer and fall. Use Beetle Spins, crickets or live worms for best results. Crappie fishing is a waste of time. Snook fishing is good in the southern half of the river. The stream also has been stocked with sunshine bass.

Webb Management Area: Marl pits have been constructed in this wildlife management area, which is 8 miles south of Punta Gorda on U.S. Highway 41. Also, a new 350-acre lake is now open for fishing Thursday through Sunday. All largemouth bass must be released, however. Ponds and lakes offer best fishing in early spring for bass and late spring and summer for bream. Both species take small spinnerbaits readily. There are no sunshine bass here and very few speckled perch.

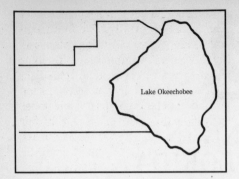

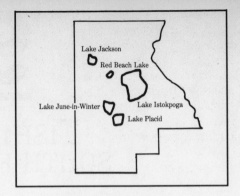

GLADES COUNTY

Lake Okeechobee: Excellent stringers of largemouth bass, bream and speckled perch come from this 448,000-acre lake. This vast lake is accessible through numerous fish camps located off U.S. highways 27 and 441. It is also an excellent fly fishing lake. Surface lures and poppers are excellent producers for largemouth bass during warm periods in December, January and February. Bedding panfish are plentiful for the cane pole fisherman during March, April, May and June on live bait. Fly rods snag their share, too. World famous crappie fishing is December through February. Live Missouri minnows and jigs work best when fished in grassy areas 3 to 6 feet deep. There are no sunshine bass in Lake Okeechobee. If you are after lunker largemouths, a special 2-hook plastic weedless worm is an excellent lure when fished in the grass during the spring months.

HIGHLANDS COUNTY

Lake Istokpoga: This shallow, tannic-stained lake is situated just off U.S. Highway 98 at Lorida. Its 27,000 acres offer outstanding fishing for bream during the spawning months of late spring and early summer. Use fly rods with poppers and rubber bugs and live bait such as crickets and worms. Bass fishing is better during the cooler months on plastic worms and crankbaits. Fish around the fish attractors. Bream fishing is fair during late spring and early summer on live bait and small artificials. There are no sunshine bass.

Lake Jackson: Don't confuse this lake with the better-known Lake Jackson near Tallahassee. This lake, east of U.S. Highway 27 in Sebring, is an excellent lake to wade and fly fish. Look for buoys that mark the fish attractors. The fishing is outstanding for drifting in open water with minnows. Area bass fishermen consider this to be one of the best largemouth lakes in Highlands County. Fish with plastic worms and crankbaits and don't overlook the fish attractors. Bream fishing is fair during late spring and early summer on live bait and small artificials. No sunshine bass fishing here.

Lakes June-in-Winter and Placid:
Near the city of Lake Placid off U.S.
Highway 27, these lakes are quite
similar in many respects. The water
quality is excellent and they are
about 3,000-acre lakes. They are both
known for bass fishing around submerged vegetation on weedless lures
during the summer. Speck fishing is
good in these two lakes during late
fall and winter. No sunshine bass
here either.

Red Beach Lake: A fish management area 1 mile northeast of the
junction of U.S. highways 98 and 27,
south of Sebring, this area offers
good bass fishing in shallow water.
The best time is during the spring
when the bass are bedding. During
summer months, find the deep holes
and fish plastic worms and deep-running lures. While Red Beach Lake is
not noted for its bream fishing, you
can catch them during the spring and
summer spawning season in shallow
water with live crickets and worms.
For good speckled perch fishing, drift
in open water with live minnows during the winter months. Also, fish the
grassy areas with minnows. There
are no sunshine bass.

bass fishing is good during the winter
months when drifting with minnows
and grass shrimp. During the summer months jigging the old river
channel can be productive. Bass fishing is fair with live shiners fished
around vegetation or free-lined under
hydrilla mats. Bream fishing is fair
during April, May and June on live
crickets, worms and artificial Beetle
Spins. The best method for catching
specks is drifting the old river channel with jigs and live Missouri minnows.

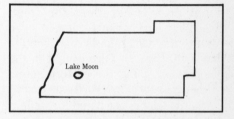

PASCO COUNTY

Lake Moon: A fish management area
6 miles east of New Port Richey on
S.R. 587, this 99-acre lake is noted
for its clear, deep water and its bass
and bream fishing. Fish during October and during early spring with live
shiners for best results. Bream fishing is excellent with grass shrimp or
on a fly rod with rubber bugs. Crappie fishing is not good in this lake.

MANATEE COUNTY

Lake Manatee: This is a fish management area that was created by
damming the east fork of the Manatee River. It is located at the junction
of state roads 675 and 64. Sunshine

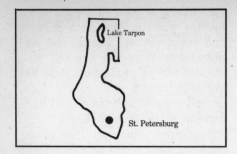

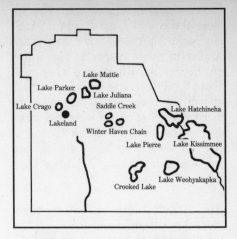

PINELLAS COUNTY

Lake Tarpon: A former state large-mouth record came from this lake 3 miles southeast of Tarpon Springs on U.S. Highway 19. This fish management area is excellent for small schooling bass when fishing in open water and using lures that imitate bait fish. Bass also are caught in the deep water along the eastern shore. Although a former record was caught here, the lake is not noted for its lunker bass fishing. However, it is an excellent lake for shellcracker fishing, especially during April when using live earthworms. Speckled perch fishing is fair during January and February. Look for the buoys that mark the fish attractors for good fishing.

POLK COUNTY

Crooked Lake: This lake with 5,000 acres of deep, clear water is south of Lake Wales off U.S. Highway 27. A public boat ramp is available to fisherman 1 mile off U.S. 27 on S.R. 630-A. Bass fishing is excellent when trolling lures or live shiners. Also, look for schooling bass. Speck fishing is excellent with live Missouri minnows, grass shrimp and artificial jigs. For nice stringers of bream, fish during the bedding season and use live crickets and worms.

Lake Crago: A fish management area created by phosphate mining, this lake is adjacent to Lake Parker off S.R. 33 in Lakeland. It is noted for its bass fishing during the bedding season, February through March, on plastic worms and live shiners. Bream angling is poor in this area, but sunshine bass can be caught in the canal leading to Lake Parker during periods of water movement created by wind or heavy rainfall. Grass shrimp are best.

Lake Hatchineha: Connected to the northwest end of Lake Kissimmee by a canal, this shallow, grassy 6,000-acre lake is excellent for fly fishermen in search of bass or bream. Late spring and early summer are best for both using this method. Fish the vegetation with plastic worms and spinnerbaits. This lake is also an excellent speck lake. Use live minnows, artificial jigs and live grass shrimp during the fall, winter and early spring. Cypress trees lining the shoreline house numerous types of wildlife such as the osprey. Several fish camps offer access: Port Hatchineha, off S.R. 542 near Lake Hamilton; Camp Mary, also off S.R. 542, and Camp Lester, which is on the canal between Hatchineha and Lake Kissimmee and can be reached off U.S. Highway 27 near Lake Wales.

Lake Juliana: This 926-acre fish management area is located north of Auburndale and west of S.R. 559. It is an outstanding speck fishing lake and is known for the large specks that are caught frequently. Most anglers drift the open water with live minnows to locate schools of specks at night. Bass fishing is excellent around the game commission's fish attractors and around other submerged structures. The best bet is to cast plastic worms and crankbaits. Bream fishing is good during the spawning season on live crickets, worms or small spinners and Bream Killers. There are no sunshine bass here.

Lake Kissimmee: Known throughout the South as an excellent bass lake, this 34,948-acre lake just south of Lake Hatchineha got a shot in the arm when it was drawn down in 1977. The drawdown stimulated growth of good vegetation and improved the fishing. Access is available at Oasis Fish Camp, on U.S. Highway 60 near Lake Wales, and Camp Mack, which is on the canal between Lake Hatchineha and Lake Kissimmee. Vast areas of shallow water with vegetation provide excellent fly rod bass

fishing. Plastic worms and surface lures such as buzz baits fished in heavy vegetation are very productive for largemouths. This lake is good year-round for bass, specks and bream. The peak time for bream fishing is April through June using Beetle Spins and fly rods. Speck fishing is good throughout the lake on live minnows and grass shrimp when drifted in open water and fished around the cattails. Night fishing is excellent for black crappie (specks), but should be attempted with caution because there are no landmarks.

Lake Mattie: A 1,078-acre fish management area located north of Auburndale and east of S.R. 559, this lake is known for its large speckled perch. The best months for speck are December and January when drifting open water with live minnows at night and using lights. Bass fishing is good around submerged stump fields and fish attractors. Plastic worms and spinnerbaits are the best lures. The stump fields are also productive for bream during the hot-weather spawning months.

Lake Parker: Look for the fish attractor buoys in this 2,272-acre fish management area northeast of Lakeland off S.R. 33. This lake has become one of the best bass fishing lakes in the area. Most of the largemouths are caught by anglers fishing the hydrilla beds or flipping cattails with plastic worms. Sunshine bass fishing is outstanding in the power plant outflow in cold months when using grass shirmp. Bream fishing is excellent during the warmer months, but speck fishing is only fair in this lake.

Lake Pierce: Many fishermen consider this to be the best lake for bass fishing in Central Florida. It is located near Dundee off S.R. 17A and offers excellent bass fishing around the hydrilla beds. Look for holes in the hydrilla and fish them with live shiners. It is also a good lake for bream and crappie fishing during the spawning seasons, but it offers no sunshine bass fishing.

Lake Weohyakapka: Better known as "Lake Walking Waters," this 7,000-acre lake is 4 miles south of U.S. Highway 60 between Yeehaw Junction and Lake Wales. It has fish attractors and offers good speck fishing during the cooler months. Drift in open water during the day and at night using live minnows. Use a nightlight when fishing at night to attract bait and fish. Bass fishing is good throughout the lake and especially around the fish attractors. Use live shiners and artificial worms for best results. It is one of the best shellcracker fishing lakes and perhaps the best for big shellcrackers (redears). Use live worms. There are no sunshine bass here.

Saddle Creek: This fish management area, created by phosphate mining, is on the northeast side of Lakeland just off U.S. Highway 92. It has swimming and playground facilities and offers good bank fishing with artificial lures that emulate shad for sunshine bass. Largemouth bass fishing is good year-round and bream angling is good.

Winter Haven Chain: This chain of nine lakes yields some of the most consistent catches of fish in the region. There is a public boat ramp off S.R. 655 south of Auburndale on Lake Lulu. Bass fishing is the best bet throughout the entire chain. Flipping is the most effective method of fishing in the darker water. Use a plastic worm or eel and rig it with a Texas rig. The lake offers something for all bass fishermen, however. Fly

fishermen, worm fishermen or live-bait fishermen will all find good bass fishing in this scenic chain. Sunshine bass fishing is good, too. Fish grass shrimp or crankbaits in the canals when the water is moving. Bream fishing is also good in all the lakes, but speck fishing is best in lakes Eloise, Howard and Hartridge. Drift with live minnows for best results. Anglers can find something hitting in one lake or another throughout the year.

Tenoroc State Reserve Fish Management Area: (not shown) This area 2 miles northeast of Lakeland consists of 1,000 acres of lakes and channels reclaimed from phosphate mining operations. Six lakes are now open for fishing with each lake having different regulations; gear restrictions, catch and release programs, bag limits and quotas on the number of boats and fishermen. However, all lakes allow unlimited catches of catfish and tilapia as well as catches of 50 panfish a day per person. Some huge bass frequent these waters. For reservations and more information, call (813) 665-8270 Thursday through Sunday between noon and 4 p.m.

The Florida Phosphate Council publishes a brochure, "A Guide to Recreation on Florida's Reclaimed Phosphate Lands," which describes eight areas in Hillsborough and Polk counties that offer a variety of outdoor recreation opportunities — including fishing. For information, write to the Information Bureau, Florida Phosphate Council, P.O Box 5530, Lakeland, Fla. 33803, or call (813) 646-8583.

Furthermore, maps listing sites for fishing, boating, picnicking and camping facilities on Lake Okeechobee, the Everglades conservation areas and the Kissimmee River chain may be obtained by writing to the South Florida Water Conservation District, P.O. Box V, West Palm Beach, Fla. 33402.

SOUTH FLORIDA
FISH CAMPS

CHARLOTTE COUNTY

Charlotte Harbor

Gasparilla Marina:
County Road 771, Placida, 33946; (813) 697-2842.
Access to Charlotte Harbor & Gulf. Ramp, bait, tackle, repairs and hoist.

Lemon Bay

Lemon Bay Ramp:
Lemon Bay Bridge, S.R. 776, Englewood.
Boat ramp.

State Beach Park:
Englewood and Shore View Drive, Englewood.
Boat ramp.

Peace River

Punta Gorda:
U.S. Highway 41 and Barron Collier Bridge.
Boat ramp.

Darst Avenue Park Ramp:
Riverside Drive and Darst Avenue, Punta Gorda.
Boat ramp.

Harbour Heights Park Ramp:
Harbour Heights and N. San Marino Drive.
Boat ramp.

Peace River Fish Camp:
29208 Snook Circle, Punta Gorda, 33950; (813) 639-2819.
Off U.S. Highway 17 north.
Five boats, living units, guides, bait, tackle, ramp (50 cents), marina, camp sites and general store.

Port Charlotte Beach Ramp:
Harbor Boulevard West.
Boat ramp.

Riverside Park Camp:
Cleveland and Riverside Drive, Punta Gorda.
Boat ramp.

Shell Creek

Shell Creek Park:
Route 23, Box 850, Punta Gorda, 33950; (813) 639-4234.
County Road 764, 10 miles from Punta Gorda.
Licenses, tackle, camping and RV facilities, bait, groceries.

DESOTO COUNTY

Peace River

Desoto Marina:
Route 3, Box 747, Arcadia, 33821; (813) 625-4407.
Tackle, boat docks, ramp, bar and grill.

Lettuce Lake Boat Ramp:
Off S.R. 761; P.O. Box 97, Ogden, 33842; (813) 494-6057.
Campsites, county boat ramp.

GLADES COUNTY

Fisheating Creek

Fisheating Creek Campground:
U.S. Highway 27, 1 mile north of S.R. 29; Box 100, Palmdale, 33944; (813) 675-1852.
Bait, boats, tackle, campsites, groceries and RV hookups.

Glades County Public Boat Lodging:
Lakeport. Boat ramp at Fisheating Creek (cannot get to lake during low water).
1 outdoor facility.

Harney Pond Canal

Harney Pond Canal:
S.R. 78 near Lakeport.
Boat ramp, public access.

Indian Prairie Canal

Indian Prairie Canal:
Boat ramp, access point to lake, no camping.

Lake Okeechobee

Big Bear Beach:
17 miles north of Moore Haven on S.R. 78 (direct access to lake).
Boat ramp.

Buckhead Ridge Marina:
S.R. 78 on Fish-Full Lake; 250 Buckhead Ridge, Okeechobee, 33472; (813) 763-2826.
Lodging, campsites, beer, groceries, ice, gas, guide, licenses, bait, tackle, boat storage, restaurant.

Calusa Lodge:
Route 2, S.R. 78, Moore Haven, 33471; (813) 946-1601.
10 boats, 4 guides, bait, 10 motors, marina, lodging, ramp, campsites, licenses.

FCD Recreation Area:
S.R. 78 at Buckhead Ridge.
Boat ramp, public use area.

O Kissimmee:
S.R. 78 and Kissimmee River; Route 4, Box 650, Okeechobee, 33472; (813) 763-4987.
Bait, fuel, boats, motors, tackle, groceries, ramp.

HARDEE COUNTY

Peace River

Gardner Boat Ramp:
Off U.S. Highway 17 south of Arcadia.
Boat ramp.

Pioneer Park Boat Ramp:
Zolfo Springs at Pioneer Park off U.S. Highway 17.
Boat ramp.

Popash Ramp:
Next to bridge on S.R. 64A east of Wauchula.
Ramp into Peace River.

HERNANDO COUNTY

Lake Lindsey

Lake Lindsey:
County Road 581 about 4 miles north of Brooksville.
Boat ramp.

Mountain Lake

Mountain Lake:
From U.S. Highway 41 to Mountain Lake Road, about 1 mile south of Spring Lake.
Boat ramp.

Silver Lake

Silver Lake:
Rital Croom Road, about 2 miles east of I-75 off S.R. 50.
Boat ramp.

Weeki Wachee River

Hernando Beach Marina:
4139 Shoal Line Blvd., Spring Hill, 33526.
S.R. 595, Hernando Beach west off S.R. 50, Weeki Wachee Springs; (904) 596-2952.
Lifts, ice, repair, full-service gas.

Boat Ramp:
S.R. 595 at Rogers Park, about 3 miles south of S.R. 50.

Withlacoochee River

Boat Ramp:
S.R. 476 in Nobleton.

Big Bass Resort:
P.O. Box 28, Istahatta, 33460; (904) 796-3784.
11 miles north of U.S. 41 from Brooksville, east on S.R. 476 to County Road 39. North for 1 mile.
Boats, cabins, motors, bait, RV campsites, ramp, dock, trailer, row boats, canoes.

HIGHLANDS COUNTY

Arbuckle Creek

Burnt Bridge Boat Ramp:
Off S.R. 621, Horse Hammock Road.
Boat ramp.

Dinner Lake

Dinner Lake Landing:
Carter Creek Road, 1½ miles east of S.R. 17, Sebring.
Boat ramp.

Public Access Ramp:
U.S. Highway 27 near ACL Railroad, north of airport and race track.
Concrete boat ramp.

Francis Lake

Francis Lake Boat Landing:
4-H Road off S.R. 621, 1 mile west of U.S. Highway 27.
Boat ramp.

Harney Pond Canal

Harney Pond Canal Launch:
S.R. 70, 8 miles east of U.S. Highway 27.
Boat ramp.

Kissimmee River

EEEE Fish Camp:
U.S. Highway 98 between Sebring and Okach; Route 1, Box 512, Lorida, 33857; (813) 763-3330
Boats, living units, tackle, bait, camping facilities, groceries and ramp.

Kissimmee River Boat Launch:
Off S.R. 70, 4 miles north on Nine-Mile-Grade, then 1½ miles east.
Boat ramp.

Kissimmee River Fishing Resort:
S.R. 70, west of Kissimmee River; Star Route 6, Box 100, Okeechobee, 33472; (813) 763-3542.
Living units, camping facilities, bait, ramp.

Lake Bonnett

Camp-n-Comfort:
2181 W. Bonnet View Road, Avon Park, 33825; (813) 385-2093.
Lodging, bait, campsites, mobile homes, apartments, ramp.

Lake Bonnett Village:
Route 1, Box 820, Avon Park, 33825.

Lake Clay

Lake Clay Boating:
Lake Clay Drive, 2 miles north of Lake Placid, 3 miles east of U.S. Highway 27.

Lake Damon

Public Ramp:
U.S. Highway 27 north of S.R. 64.
Concrete ramp.

Lake Grassy

Lake Placid Campground:
1801 U.S. Highway 27 south; P.O. Box 162, Route 3, Lake Placid, 33852; (813) 465-2934.
Boats, living units, camping facilities, ramp. No pets.

Lake Istokpoga

Cypress Isle Fish Camp:
East of Lake Placid off U.S. Highway 27 on County Road 621; Route 5, Box 552, Lake Placid, 33852; (813) 465-5241.
Boats, living units, tackle, bait, camping facilities.

Mallard Mobile Home Park:
P.O. Box 430, U.S. Highway Highway 98, Lorida, 33857.
Boat ramp, recreation hall, full RV hookup and guide service.

Lake Istokpoga Boat Landing:
South end of lake.
Public access.

Lake Jackson

City of Sebring Boat Landing:
Elk's Beach, Veterans Memorial Park, west side Lake Jackson.

Public Access:
Off U.S. Highway 27 South.
Public beach, picnic area, gas, bait, dock.

Lake Josephine

Kemps Resort:
3 miles west of U.S. Highway 27 on S.R. 621; Rural Route 1, Box 110F, Lake Placid, 33852; (813) 465-2952.
Boats, tackle, bait, groceries.

Lake Josephine Landing:
A half mile north of Josephine Road on the west side of Lake Josephine.

Lake Lelia

Lake Lelia Landing:
1 mile south of Avon Park, a quarter mile east of U.S. Highway 27.

Lake Letta

Lake Letta Landing:
S.R. 17, 3 miles south of Avon Park.

Lake Lotela

Lake Lotela Landing:
Highlands Avenue, 1 mile south of Avon Park.

Lake Pythisa

Public Ramp:
U.S. Highway 27, 1 mile south of Avon Park.

Lake Sebring

Lake Sebring Landing:
S.R. 17, 4 miles south of Avon Park.

Little Red Water Lake

Boat Landing:
S.R. 17, 1 mile north of U.S. Highway 98.

HILLSBOROUGH COUNTY

Manatee River

Fort Hammer:
Fort Hammer Road, off U.S. Highway 301, Parrish.
Public ramp.

Randall's Fish Camp:
7204 Harney Road, Tampa, 33617; (813) 988-9780.
Licenses, tackle, bait, ramp, groceries.

MANATEE COUNTY

Braden River

Fort Hammer Boat Ramp:
Fort Hammer Rd. off U.S. Highway 301 from Parrish on Manatee River.
Picnic area, concrete dock, ramp at end of road.

Jiggs Landing:
Off S.R. 70; 6106 Braden River Road, Bradenton, 34203; (813) 756-6745.
Boat rentals, tackle, bait, snacks, cold drinks.

Linger Lodge:
Off S.R. 70 and 63rd Street; 7205 Linger Lodge Road, Bradenton, 34202; (813) 755-2757.
Travel trailer spaces, swimming, shuffleboard, horseshoes, laundromat, ramp, ice, beer.

PASCO COUNTY

Lake Jovitta

San Antonio Public Beach:
Off S.R. 52, west of Dade City.
Ramp.

Moon Lake

Cypress Creek Campgrounds:
Route 8, Box 831, Lutz, 33549; (813) 949-6934.
RV sites, no fishing facilities.

Public Beach and Park:
Off S.R. 587, northeast of New Port Richey.
Free public ramp.

PINELLAS COUNTY

Lake Seminole

Bass Fishing Heaven:
U.S. Highway Alt. 19; 8801 Seminole Blvd., Seminole, 33542; (813) 392-4817.
Motors, boats, guides, tackle, bait, ramp, boat rentals.

Lake Tarpon

The Tarpon Turtle:
S.R. 582, half mile east of U.S. Highway 19; 1513 Lake Tarpon Ave., Tarpon Springs, 33589; (813) 934-3696.
Ramp, gas, boat slips for rent, restaurant, cottages.

POLK COUNTY

Crooked Lake

Bob's Landing Mobile Home Park and Marina:
Ohlinger Street, Babson Park, 33827; (813) 638-1912.
Boats, gas, ramp, oil, covered boat slips.

Eagle Lake

Eagle Lake Boat Ramp and Park:
Eagle Avenue, Eagle Lake.
Tables and beach.

Lake Kissimmee

Camp Lester:
16 miles east of Lake Wales off U.S. Highway 60; 14400 Reese Drive, Lake Wales, 33853; (813) 696-1123.
Guides, licenses, tackle, bait, camping facilities, rental cabins, swimming pool, ice, ramp.

Grape Hammock:
Off U.S. Highway 60; 1400 Grape Hammock Road, Lake Wales, 33853; (813) 692-1500.
Boats, bait, guides, camping facilities, ramp, and cottages.

Camp Mack:
14900 Camp Mack Road, Lake Wales, 33853; (813) 696-1108.
Boats, living units, tackle, licenses, bait, camping facilities, ramp.

Outdoor Resort River Ranch:
Off U.S. Highway 60 on Kissimmee River; 24700 U.S. Highway 60 East, Lake Wales, 33853; (813) 692-1321.
Bait, tackle, boats, motors, licenses, guides, motel, RV, tenting, cottages, efficiencies, grocery store.

Shady Oaks:
Off U.S. Highway 60; 1800 Shady Oaks Road, Lake Wales, 33853; (813) 692-1261.
Tackle, bait, snack bar, ramp, groceries, RV hookups, gas and oil, rental cabins.

The Oasis:
25601 U.S. Highway 60 East, Lake Wales, 33853; (813) 692-1594.
Boats, living units, guides, licenses, tackle, bait, groceries, camping facilities, ramp, self-contained trailers, RV hookups, gas.

Public Landing:
U.S. Highway 60, east of Lake Wales at Kissimmee River Bridge above dam entrance.

Lake Alfred

Lake Alfred Boat Ramp:
Nekoma Street, Lions Park, Lake Alfred.

Lake Annie

Lake Annie Boat Launch:
S.R. 70, 1 mile west of U.S. Highway 27.

Lake Arbuckle

Public Landing:
Lake Arbuckle Road (off East Lake Reedy Drive), east of Frostproof on S.R. 630.
Guides, camping facilities.

Lake Ariana

Lake Ariana Boat Ramp:
Lake Ariana Boulevard and Lake Alfred Road, Auburndale.

Lake Ariana Boat Ramp and Park:
Lake Ariana Boulevard and Dixie Highway, Auburndale.
Adjacent to beach.

Lake Arietta

Lake Arietta Boat Ramp:
Gapway Road, Auburndale.

Lake Buffum

Lake Buffum Boat Ramp:
West Buffum Drive, west on Babson Park Alturas Road.

Lake Cannon

Lake Cannon County Park:
Lake Cannon Drive, Winter Haven.
Ramp, tables, beach.

Lake Elbert

Lake Elbert Boat Ramp:
Lake Elbert Drive, N.E., Winter Haven.

Lake Garfield

Lake Garfield Boat Ramp:
Lake Garfield Road, S.R. 655.

Lake Haines

Lake Haines Boat Ramp:
East Haines Boulevard, Lake Alfred.

Lake Hancock

Public Landing:
S.R. 540 at Saddle Creek Bridge, between U.S. Highway 98 and Spirit Lake Road.

Lake Hatchineha

Port Hatchineha Marina:
15050 Hatchineha Road, Haines City, 33844; (813) 439-2376.
Licenses, snacks, ice, beer, bait, restaurant, motel, ramp, gas, tackle.

Lake Howard

Lake Howard City Pier:
Lake Howard Drive, Winter Haven.
Two ramps.

Lake Jessie

Lake Jessie Boat Ramp:
Biltmore Drive off S.R. 544 and 29th Street, Winter Haven.

Lake Juliana

Fish Haven Lodge:
Route 1, Box 1, Chipman Lane, Auburndale, 33823; (813) 984-1183.
Cottages, mobile home park, fishing pier, swimming, travel trailer spaces.

Lundy's Fish Camp:
Route 1, Box 600, Auburndale, 33823; (813) 984-1144.
Cottages, fishing pier, bait, trailer park, swimming pool, beach, boats, ramp.

Lake Livingston

Public Landing:
South of Frostproof on Alternate 27, 33843.

Lake Lowry

Oak Harbor Campground:
West Lake Lowry Road, west side of lake; P.O. Box 507, Lake Alfred, 33850; (813) 956-1341.
RV and mobile home park, boat ramp. Closed from May to October.

Lake Marion

Shady Cove Fishing Resort:
Off S.R. 544; 1090 Shady Cove E., Haines City, 33844; (813) 422-2015.
Boats, tackle, bait, camping facilities, ramp.

St. Clair's Lake Marion Resort:
9696 St. Clair Road, Haines City, 33844; (813) 422-4740.
Tackle, mobile home spaces, ramp, motors, boats.

Lake Pierce

Cherry Pocket:
Off Alternate 27; 3100 Canal Road, Lake Wales, 33853; (813) 439-9854.
Cabins, grocery store, bar, boats, RV lots, tackle, bait, ramp.

Jennings Resort:
Off Alternate 27; 3600 Jennings Road, Lake Wales, 33853; (813) 439-3811.
Boats, living units, tackle, bait, camping facilities, groceries, ramp, motors.

Public Landing:
Timberland Road, east of Lake Wales, west side of Lake Pierce.

Lake Reedy

Public Landing:
Lake Arbuckle Road, east of Frostproof off S.R. 630, west side of Lake Reedy.
Camping facilities.

Public Landing:
Camp Sheppard Road, south of Frostproof, on Alternate 27.

Lake Rochelle

Lake Rochelle Boat Ramp:
U.S. Highway 17-92, half mile east of Winter Haven on Lake Alfred Road, Lake Alfred.

Lake Rosalie

Camp Rosalie:
3000 Camp Rosalie Road, Lake Wales, 33853; (813) 696-2662.
Ramp.

Public Landing:
Camp Pennington Road, east of Lake Wales off U.S. Highway 60, south side of Lake Rosalie.
Camping facilities.

Lake Shipp

Lake Shipp County Park:
S.R. 655 from Auburndale, west side of Lake Shipp.
Ramp, tables, beach.

Lake Summitt

Lake Summitt-Lake Eloise Boat Ramp:
Summitt Drive, Winter Haven.

Lake Swoope

Lake Swoope Boat Ramp:
Rochelle Drive, Lake Alfred.

Lake Tracy

Lake Tracy Boat Ramp:
McKay Drive off U.S. Highway 17-92, Haines City, 33844.

Lake Wales Lake

Public Landing:
East side of Lake Wales.

Middle Lake Hamilton

Paradise Island Campground:
3 miles south of Haines City; 2900 S. U.S. Highway 27, Haines City, 33844; (813) 439-1350.
Swimming pool, travel trailers, camp spaces, tackle, groceries, boat ramp, rowboats, paddle boats, canoes and three fishing docks.

Tiger Lake

Camp Tiger:
Off U.S. Highway 60; 1731 Sam Keen Road, Lake Wales, 33853; (813) 692-1577.
Tackle, bait, camping facilities, ramp, grocery store.

SOUTH FLORIDA FISHING BAROMETER

Month	Largemouth Bass	Black Crappie	Sunshine Bass	Bream
January	Fair-good	Excellent	Good	Poor
February	Excellent	Excellent	Good	Poor
March	Excellent	Good	Good	Fair
April	Good	Fair	Fair	Fair-good
May	Good	Poor	Poor	Good
June	Fair-good	Poor	Poor	Good
July	Fair-good	Poor	Poor	Good
August	Fair-good	Poor	Poor	Good
September	Fair-good	Poor	Poor-fair	Good
October	Fair-good	Poor-fair	Poor-fair	Poor-fair
November	Fair	Fair-good	Excellent	Poor
December	Fair	Excellent	Excellent	Poor

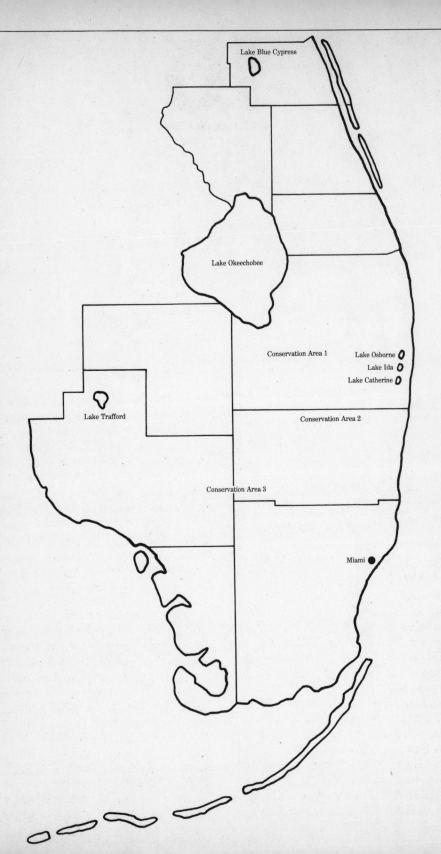

Lake Blue Cypress

Lake Okeechobee

Conservation Area 1

Lake Osborne

Lake Ida

Lake Catherine

Lake Trafford

Conservation Area 2

Conservation Area 3

Miami

10

FISHING IN THE EVERGLADES

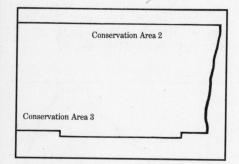

Conservation Area 2

Conservation Area 3

BROWARD COUNTY

Conservation Area 2: This area consists of 210 square miles of Everglades marsh connected with perimeter canals. Largemouth bass, bluegills, redears and warmouths are abundant along with some snook and tarpon. Main points of entry are the Loxahatchee Recreation Area on S.R. 827 off U.S. Highway 441 at the Palm Beach-Broward county line, and at the Sawgrass Recreation Area on U.S. Highway 27, 2 miles north of Andytown, just north of Alligator Alley (S.R. 84). A drawdown has made for excellent bass and bream fishing

in the canals. For bass, use plastic worms during the day and surface lures or crankbaits early in the morning or late in the afternoon. Bream bed during the warmer months and offer sport for the fly fisherman who uses sinking bugs, or to cane pole fisherman who prefer to use live crickets or redworms. Catfish are abundant also and can be lured with dead bait such as cut bait, shrimp or liver fished on the bottom of the canals.

Conservation Area 3: This area covers 730 square miles of Everglades wetlands bordered by a canal system. The most sought after sport fish are bass, bluegills, shellcrackers (redears) and warmouths. The main access points are the Everglades Holiday Park on U.S. Highway 27, 6 miles south of Andytown, and Mack's Fish Camp on Danell Lane off Krome Avenue, a half mile south of U.S. 27. Most of the fishing in this area is limited to the canals along Alligator Alley, the Miami Canal and other systems. However, when water levels are high enough, the interior of the area can be fished by airboat. Use plastic worms in the canals for bass. Live shiners work well, too. Bream will take live crickets, worms or artificial jigs and spinners.

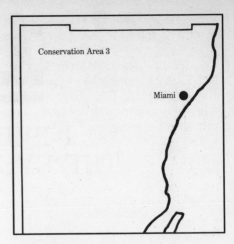

DADE COUNTY

Conservation Area 3: Dade County launching sites for this area, which is listed in the Broward County entry, are on U.S. Highway 41 west of Miami at the S-12-C, S-12-D and S-333 water management structures, and the Krome Avenue recreation site on Krome Avenue (S.R. 27) 1 mile north of U.S. Highway 27.

COLLIER COUNTY

Lake Trafford: A 1,500-acre natural body of water, this lake offers excellent sport fishing for largemouth bass, bream, speckled perch and catfish. One entry point is at Lake Trafford Marina, on Lake Trafford Road off S.R. 29 near Immokalee. Boat channels have been cut through this weed-infested lake. The weeds make for good bass fishing, especially during the spring when the females are bedding. Live shiners are good bait. So are plastic worms and weedless spoons. Trafford is also an excellent lake for shellcrackers during the late spring bedding season. Use live worms for the redears and fish on or near the bottom.

HENDRY COUNTY

Lake Okeechobee: Florida's largest lake, this vast body of water spans 730 square miles. Its waters offer excellent fishing for largemouth bass, specks, bream and catfish. It is known widely as one of Florida's best fishing lakes. Hendry County access points to the lake include Angler's Marina, 910 Okeechobee Blvd., Clewiston; Roland Martin Marina, 920 East Delmonte, Clewiston; Jolly Roger Marina, U.S. Highway 27, Clewiston; and public launching ramps and city docks on Okeechobee Boulevard. Lake Okeechobee's fish population moves around from one season to another and most people find it helpful to hire a local guide, at least on the first trip. Bass hit best in late winter and early spring when the fish are bedding in the needlegrass and peppergrass flats. Use plastic worms or weedless spoons, or use live shiners, the best natural bait. Bream fishing really gets going in late spring. The shorelines of the lake's canals are often lined with bluegill beds. Try a fly rod and a small top-water popper for great fun and sport. A sinking spider fly will do the trick also. Catfish are easy to catch if you fish on the bottom with live worms, dead shrimp or cut bait. Snook, tarpon, jack crevalle and other saltwater species also venture into the lake. For speckled perch, fish the coldest months of winter for best results. Local fisherman, however, know where to catch them throughout the year. Most of the camps have fishing guides. I recommend you use one. It's worth the expense until you learn where to fish.

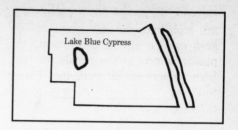

INDIAN RIVER COUNTY

Lake Blue Cypress: This 6,555-acre lake, bordered by marsh and cypress swamp, offers good fishing for large-mouth bass, bluegills and shellcrackers along with warmouths, spotted sunfish, speckled perch and catfish. Sunshine bass were stocked in 1976. It has only one access point: Blue Cypress Fish Camp, Blue Cypress Grade, 4 miles off S.R. 60, about 12 miles east of Yeehaw Junction from Florida's Turnpike, or 25 miles west of Vero Beach. Blue Cypress is best known for its speckled perch, which are caught in abundance by anglers drifting to locate a school, then anchoring to fish. Sunshine bass are taken in this manner, too. Use a live Missouri minnow or a small jig. Largemouth bass fishing is good in areas with structures or cover such as the cypress shoreline. Bluegills will hit live bait such as crickets or worms during summer months. Flyrod fishing is good then, too.

MARTIN COUNTY, OKEECHOBEE COUNTY

Lake Okeechobee: See Hendry County. However, other access points are in Martin County — J and S Fish Camp, 17 miles south of Okeechobee City on U.S. Highway 441, and in Okeechobee County at Okee-Tantie Fish Camp, Taylor Creek East and

West, Barlow's, the Fijian, OKissimmee, Captain Bill's and Butch's fish camps.

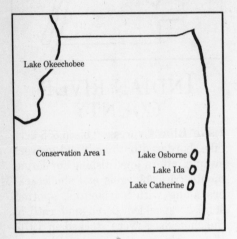

PALM BEACH COUNTY

Lake Okeechobee: See Hendry County. Local access points in addition to those listed in Hendry County include Slim's Fish Camp, S.R. 717, Belle Glade; J-Mark, S.R. 717; Pahokee Harbor Pier at Pahokee State Park; and Belle Glade municipal docks.

Conservation Area 1: Fishing generally is limited to the canal system, but there's plenty of good fishing for bass, bream and catfish. This 221-square-mile portion of the Everglades is managed by the U.S. Fish and Wildlife Service, which sees to it that there is good fishing for largemouths, bluegills, redears, sunfish, warmouths and catfish. Access is at the Loxahatchee Refuge Headquarters off U.S. Highway 441 between Boynton Beach Road (804) and Delray Beach Road (806); the Loxahatchee Refuge ramp at the 20-mile bend on S.R. 80; and the Loxahatchee Recreation Area, S.R. 827 at U.S. Highway 441 near the Palm

Beach-Broward line. Loxahatchee is also a good place to see alligators while you fish. Largemouth bass will hit crankbaits and plastic worms, especially during early spring, which just happens to be the best time to fish for them. Bream hit crickets, worms and artificial poppers. Catfish like dead bait fished on the bottom.

Lake Osborne: There is good fishing in this 356-acre lake for largemouth bass, bream and catfish. Good sunshine bass fishing also is available from October to February. To get to the lake, which is within John Prince Park near Lake Worth, exit Interstate 95 at 6th Avenue north of Lantana Road. The lake is used heavily by water-skiers, fishermen, pleasure boaters, swimmers and campers. Fishing is good, however, for largemouth and sunshine bass, catfish and bream. For bass, use plastic worms to fish early and late — even at night. Cast cut shrimp from the bridges and fish on bottom at night for good results, especially at the Sixth Avenue and Lantana bridges. Bream and speckled perch will hit live minnows, jigs or poppers. The main problem with fishing Osborne, Lake Ida or Lake Catherine is getting away from the people. Try night fishing, especially during the summer.

Lake Ida: This 150-acre lake has a good population of largemouth bass, bream and catfish along with sunshine bass. It is within Lake Ida Park in Delray Beach. To get there, exit I-95 at Atlantic Boulevard and go north on Congress Avenue.

Lake Catherine: This 15-acre lake is in Palm Beach Gardens. Here you will find largemouth bass, sunshine bass, bream and catfish. The lake has a boat ramp only and connects with lakes Ida and Osborne. To get there, exit I-95 at North Palm Beach. Go north on MacArthur Boulevard. It is best to consult the local tackle shop operators if you are planning to fish the many canals in the area.

EVERGLADES
FISH CAMPS

BROWARD COUNTY

Conservation Area 3

Everglades Holiday Park:
Corner U.S. 27 and Griffin Road
21940 Griffin Road, Fort Lauderdale, 33332;
(305) 434-8111
Free ramps, groceries, bait, fuel, ice, camp-sites with electricity and water available; boats with or without motors. 45-minute airboat tours from 9 a.m. to 5 p.m., includes zoo and alligator wrestling show.

Conservation Area 2

Sawgrass Recreation Area:
S.R. 84 to U.S. 27, north 2 miles, on the right.
P.O. Box 291620, Davie, 33329; (305) 389-0202.
Ramp, bait, licenses, fuel, guides, boat stor-age, snack bar, dump station, airboat rides, boats with or without motors, camping and ca-noes.

COLLIER COUNTY

Lake Trafford

Lake Trafford Marina:
6001 Lake Trafford Road (off State Road 29), Immokalee, 33934; (813) 657-2401.
Boat ramp, ice, bathroom facilities, bait, guide service, 4.7-acre campground with elec-tricity and A/C; boats with or without motors, cable TV.

DADE COUNTY

Conservation Area 3

Milton Thompson Park:
16665 Krome Ave., Hialeah, 33010, 2 miles south of Okeechobee Road; (305) 821-5122.
29-acre campground, including three lakes available only to campers; 45 sites with elec-tricity and water; 30 sites without electricity, laundry, showers, groceries and public boat ramp across from park on west side of S.R. 997. Open Nov. 1 to May 1; canal fishing also available.

GLADES COUNTY

Lake Okeechobee

Buckhead Ridge Marina:
S.R. 78-B, Okeechobee, 33474, about 8 miles from Okeechobee City; (813) 763-2826.
Lodging, campsites, gas, oil, boats, ramps, bait, tackle, restaurant, rec. hall, showers, laundry, motor repair.

Wanda's Marina and Camp:
Rt. 2, Box 400, Moore Haven, 33471; (813) 946-1306.
On S.R. 78 between Moore Haven and Okee-chobee near Lake Port.
Complete marina, boats, drinks, ice, bait, tackle, lodging, campsites, wet and dry dock-age.

Twin Palms Camp:
Rt. 6, Box 885, Okeechobee, 33474.
On U.S. 78 between Moore Haven and Okeechobee; (813) 946-0977.
Bait, tackle, ramp, gas, licenses, cold drinks, groceries, lodging, RV park, LP gas, guide ser-vice and bird tours.

Uncle Joe's Marina and Motel:
Rt. 3, Box 221, Moore Haven, 33471.
S.R. 720, off U.S. 27; between Clewiston and Moore Haven; (813) 983-9421.
Tackle, bait, bar, groceries, gas and restaurant, efficiency cabins with A/C and TV, boats and guide service.

Fisherman's Village Marina:
Box 311, Moore Haven, 33471; (813) 946-0722.
First street north off U.S. 27.
Tackle, bait, gas, oil, props, sales and service.

Big Bass Lodge:
Route 2, Box 120, Moore Haven, 33471; (813) 946-1707.
Lakeport off S.R. 78 and County Road 721.
Guide service, efficiency apartments, ramp, tackle, bait, gas, beer and boats.

Fisheating Bay Village:
11 miles north of S.R. 78; (813) 946-1669.
Guide service, mobile home park, campgrounds, ramp, fish house, pool

Calusa Lodge:
Route 2, Highway 78, Moore Haven, 33471; (813) 946-0544
Restaurant and lounge, guide service, lodging, boats, marina, tackle, bait, RV park and campground.

Lykes Fisheating Creek Campgrounds:
P.O. Box 100, Palmdale, 33944; (813) 675-1852.
Campsites, horseback riding (weekends), stalls, tackle, ice, groceries and canoeing.

Brighton Camparina:
Rural Route 6, Box 770, Okeechobee, 33474.
Off U.S. 721 on Brighton Seminole Indian Reservation; (813) 763-8531.
Travel trailer and RV park, store, laundry, recreation room, playground, pool, full hookups for trailers, ramp and private lake for registered guests only, miniature golf.

HENDRY COUNTY

Lake Okeechobee

Angler's Marina:
910 Okeechobee Blvd., Clewiston, 33440; (813) 983-7330.
3 blocks off U.S. 27.
Free ramp, licenses, bait, ice, tackle, guide service, fuel, groceries, motel on premises, 56 trailer and campsites and boats (with or without motors), covered boat dockage.

Jolly Roger Marina and Fish Camp:
1095 East U.S. 27, Clewiston, 33440; (813) 983-7402.
Ramp, licenses, bait, ice, fuel, guides, food, sundries, marine supplies, propeller reconditioning service and boats (with or without motors), covered boat slips, Mercury and Evinrude sales and service.

Roland Martin Marina:
920 East Delmonte Ave., Clewiston, 33440; (813) 983-8930.
Fuel, tackle, ice, bait, shiners, guides, covered slips, snacks, motels nearby, campsites and boats (with or without motors). Open 5 a.m. to 6 p.m.

INDIAN RIVER COUNTY

Blue Cypress Lake

Middleton Fish Camp:
21704 73rd Manor, Vero Beach, 32960; (305) 562-9971.
Blue Cypress Grade, 4 miles off State Road 60.
Ramp, licenses, bait, ice, fuel, campsites, rental trailers, guide and boats (with motors).

MARTIN COUNTY

Lake Okeechobee

J and S Fish Camp:
Route 1, Box 1340, Okeechobee, 33474; (305) 597-9938.
17 miles south of Okeechobee on U.S. 441
Ramp, bait, fuel, cabins, boats, screened-in patio bar, Sunday fish fry 3 p.m.

OKEECHOBEE COUNTY

Lake Okeechobee

O Kissimmee Fish Camp:
Route 4, Box 650, Okeechobee, 33474; (813) 763-4987.
U.S. 78 West at the Kissimmee River
Bait, fuel, ramp, tackle, groceries, campsites (full hookups), cabins, and boats (with or without motors).

Okee-tantie Recreation Area:
10430 U.S. 78 West, Okeechobee, 33474; (813) 763-2622.

6 miles south of Okeechobee.

Free ramp, bait, ice, fuel, licenses, shower and toilet facilities, 215-acre campground. Restaurant and lounge.

Taylor Creek Lodge (East and West):
2730 U.S. 441, S.E., Okeechobee, 33474; (813) 763-4417.

South on 441 to the dike, left at red light; 2 miles down on right (before bridge).

Ramp, bait, sundries, fuel, licenses, toilet and shower facilities, RV sites, LP gas, beer, camping lots, cabins and boats (with motors), pontoon and boat rentals.

Barlow's Fish Camp:
Route 1, Box 1196, Okeechobee, 33472; (813) 763-9853.

U.S. 441, 12 miles south of Okeechobee.

Paved ramp, bait, soda, snacks, campsites, cabins, trailers, boats (with or without motors) and guide service.

Captain Bill's Fish Camp:
3201 S.E. 33rd Terrace, Okeechobee, 33474; (813) 763-4443.

Off U.S. 441, 10 minutes from town, 5 minutes to lake off Taylor Creek.

Ramp, fuel, bait, tackle, licenses, ice, cabins, boat rental (with or without motors), beer and wine lounge, efficiencies, apartments, fishing guide, and covered boat stalls. No pets.

Butch's Fish Camp:
Box 752, Okeechobee, 33474; (813) 763-8262.

One mile south of Taylor Creek on U.S. 441.

Travel trailer and mobile trailer sites, boat storage, direct access to lake, ramp, ice, sodas, beer, snacks, no boat rentals; waterfront tavern.

PALM BEACH COUNTY

Loxahatchee National Refuge
(Conservation Area 1)

Loxahatchee Recreation Area:
Route 1, Box 642-S, Pompano Beach, 33060; (305) 426-2474.

Lox Road off U.S. 441 at Palm Beach-Broward county line

Free boat ramp, bait, ice, licenses, tackle and boats (with or without motors), airboat rides.

Lake Okeechobee

Slim's Fish Camp:
P.O. Drawer 250, Belle Glade, 33430; (305) 996-3268 or -3844.

S.R. 717, Torry Island

Free ramp, bait, tackle, groceries, gas and boats (with or without motors). Sales and service on Evinrude outboard motors.

J-Mark Fish Camp:
P.O. Box 841, Belle Glade, 33430; (305) 996-5357.

State Road 717, Torry Island

Free ramp, bait, fuel, tackle, licenses, covered dock, guide service, boats (with motors), and apartments.

Pahokee Marina Pier:
171 N. Lake Ave., Pahokee, 33476; (305) 924-7600.

Three blocks east of U.S. 441 in Pahokee

Boat dockage, ramps, camping, electricity, bait, tackle, ice and groceries.

EVERGLADES FISHING BAROMETER

Month	Largemouth Bass	Black Crappie	Sunshine Bass	Bream
January	Excellent	Excellent	Excellent	Good
February	Excellent	Excellent	Good	Good
March	Excellent	Excellent	Good	Excellent
April	Good	Good	Good	Excellent
May	Good	Fair	Fair	Excellent
June	Good	Fair	Fair	Excellent
July	Good	Fair	Fair	Excellent
August	Good	Fair	Fair	Excellent
September	Excellent	Good	Excellent	Excellent
October	Excellent	Good	Excellent	Good
November	Excellent	Good	Excellent	Good
December	Excellent	Excellent	Excellent	Good

The fishing barometer charts are the result of studies and survey of fishing success conducted by commission biologists. Weather conditions and other factors can improve or reduce your chances of success at any given time.

11

FISH ATTRACTORS

As my wife and I drifted various sections of Lake Monroe, a popular speckled perch lake in the St. Johns River waterway near Sanford, the specks were flat out refusing to take our Missouri minnows. We reeled in our lines and searched for the buoys that marked one of two fish attractors on the lake. We found the buoys just off the main channel as we headed toward Sanford from the Interstate 4 bridge. We put out our lines once again and started drifting. In a short time we had strung up more than a dozen big speckled perch.

Our lines snagged the brushy fish attractors several times and we lost a few hooks — but losing a few rigs is worth a mess of specks anytime. It didn't take long to convince us that fish attractors are worthwhile and can increase your catches.

What is a fish attractor? If you were fishing salt water, they would be called artificial reefs. Attractors in fresh water usually consist of automobile tires or brush anchored with concrete blocks. The attractors concentrate fish in one area so that anglers can reduce the time they spend searching for fish. They attract largemouth bass, bluegills, shellcrackers and speckled perch.

Why do they attract fish? They provide cover where fish can hide from predators. Second, they provide attachment surfaces for aquatic insects and other fish food organisms. Jon Buntz, a commission biologist, said more attractors are being placed in Florida's lakes. At last count, 156 attractors had been placed in selected lakes throughout the state. The commission began the program in 1977 and marked each attractor with a U.S. Coast Guard approved floating buoy. The buoys are white, black and orange and have the Florida Game and Fresh Water Fish Commission emblem on them.

Located strategically so as not to interfere with swimming, water-skiing or other water sports, the attractors cover an area of 100 feet by 100 feet and are located at least 4 feet below the water's surface. They are usually installed in open water areas that lack suitable cover for fish.

Check the map to see if fish attractors are in the lakes you plan to fish. If they are, they're sure to increase your catches.

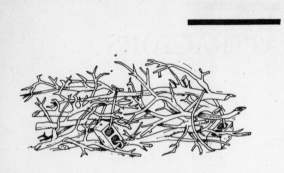

Brushy fish attractor anchored with concrete blocks

Fish attractor buoy

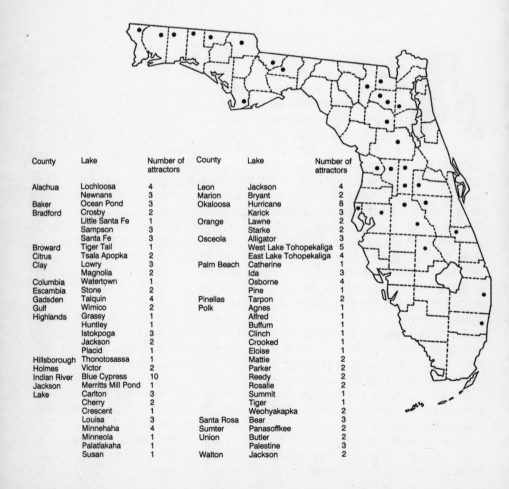

County	Lake	Number of attractors	County	Lake	Number of attractors
Alachua	Lochloosa	4	Leon	Jackson	4
	Newnans	3	Marion	Bryant	2
Baker	Ocean Pond	3	Okaloosa	Hurricane	8
Bradford	Crosby	2		Karick	3
	Little Santa Fe	1	Orange	Lawne	2
	Sampson	3		Starke	2
	Santa Fe	3	Osceola	Alligator	3
Broward	Tiger Tail	1		West Lake Tohopekaliga	5
Citrus	Tsala Apopka	2		East Lake Tohopekaliga	4
Clay	Lowry	3	Palm Beach	Catherine	1
	Magnolia	2		Ida	3
Columbia	Watertown	1		Osborne	4
Escambia	Stone	2		Pine	1
Gadsden	Talquin	4	Pinellas	Tarpon	2
Gulf	Wimico	2	Polk	Agnes	1
Highlands	Grassy	1		Alfred	1
	Huntley	1		Buffum	1
	Istokpoga	3		Clinch	1
	Jackson	2		Crooked	1
	Placid	1		Eloise	1
Hillsborough	Thonotosassa	1		Mattie	2
Holmes	Victor	2		Parker	2
Indian River	Blue Cypress	10		Reedy	2
Jackson	Merritts Mill Pond	1		Rosalie	2
Lake	Carlton	3		Summit	1
	Cherry	2		Tiger	1
	Crescent	1		Weohyakapka	2
	Louisa	3	Santa Rosa	Bear	3
	Minnehaha	4	Sumter	Panasoffkee	2
	Minneola	1	Union	Butler	2
	Palatlakaha	1		Palestine	3
	Susan	1	Walton	Jackson	2

12

RULES AND REGULATIONS

f you are caught fishing Florida's waters without a fishing license, be prepared to come up with $90, which seems to be the standard fine. All anglers are required to carry a valid fishing license stamp with these exceptions.

1. Florida residents who are 65 or older. However, they must carry a senior citizen hunting and fishing certificate. It is free and can be obtained from county tax collectors.

2. Those residents who are certified as totally and permanently disabled. They can get a similar certificate.

3. Residents who have proof they have been accepted by Health and Rehabilitative Services as a client for retardation services.

4. Children younger than 16.

5. Those who fish in a private pond.

6. Military personnel who are home on leave (Florida residents must have leave papers) for 30 days or less.

7. Those who have a Series RC (Resident-Commercial) fishing license stamp are not required to buy a license of another series.

8. Anyone fishing with cane poles and live or natural bait in the counties where they live. Non-commercial handlines are permitted also. However, anyone fishing in Fish Management Areas with any device must have a license.

Who is a Florida resident? Anyone who has lived in Florida for six continuous months, or has proof of an established predominant Florida residence. Also military personnel stationed in the state and those enrolled in a Florida university or college.

What is a private pond? According to the fish commission, this means any man-made pond of 20 acres or less constructed for the primary purpose of fishing. It must also be entirely within the owner's property line.

How much does a Florida fishing license cost? If you are a hunter and fisherman, you may want to buy a Resident Series AK fishing and hunting combination license for $17. If you just want the fishing license, get the Series AB Resident 12-month fishing license for $7.

Non-resident licenses cost more. A Series B annual fishing license is $25. A Series F 10-day license is $10.

In addition to the license stamp fees mentioned above, tax collectors are entitled to an issuance fee of $1 and their subagents are entitled to 50 cents. Fishing licenses can be purchased from county tax collectors and from most tackle shops and marinas.

Where does the fishing license money go? Revenues go into the State Game Trust Fund, which provides almost 40 percent of the commission's annual budget each year. The money is used to preserve and enhance the state's freshwater fish and wildlife resources.

What are the bag limits on freshwater game fish?

1. Largemouth (black) bass	10
2. White bass	30
3. Chain pickerel	15
4. Panfish	50
(bluegill, speckled perch, shellcracker, warmouth and red-finned pickerel individually or in total)	
5. Sunshine bass	10
6. Striped bass	6

What is the total possession limit for the above fish? Two days' bag limit after the first day of fishing except for striped bass, which have a total possession limit of 6.

What are the minimum length requirements? Of those mentioned above only the striped bass has a minimum length of 15 inches.

What are the gear restrictions? The gamefish listed above may be taken by hook and line only and may not be sold.

There may be limit variations in fish management areas or local waters. Check with your local or regional fish commission office.

13

CONCLUSION

I
n this book, I have tried to list Florida's gamefish, where and when they can be caught throughout the state and what kinds of lures and live baits they will hit best. Fishing tips and recipes were provided to make your outings more enjoyable. I have tried to bring you up to date on Florida fishing records and rules and regulations. It is my hope that wherever you go in the state with fishing rod or cane pole, this book will assist you in catching fish.

Don't be too proud to hire a fishing guide, especially during your first trip to a strange area. And don't hesitate to ask a local veteran angler or tackle shop operator where the fish were biting yesterday and where they're likely to hit best today. With this book, an inquisitive mind and a little luck, may you never come home with an empty stringer.

I hope that you have as much fun as my sons and I have had during the past 25 years or so of fishing Florida's waters from the Panhandle to the Everglades.

INDEX

Everglades

Conservation Area 1, 114
Conservation Area 2, 111
Conservation Area 3, 111, 112
Lake Blue Cypress, 113
Lake Catherine, 114
Lake Ida, 114
Lake Okeechobee, 112, 113, 114
Lake Osborne, 114
Lake Trafford, 112

F

Fish

Attractors, 121-122
Bag limits, 126
Cleaning, 24-25
Cooking, 29-31
Filleting, 26-27
Hook sizes, 16
Length requirements, 126
Licenses, 125, 126
Line maintenance, 40
Mounting, 39
Recipes, 32-35
Storage, 24
Terms, 16
Tips, 37-40

Fish camps

Northwest, 54-58
Northeast, 70,71
Central, 84-92
South, 102-107
Everglades, 116-118

Fishing barometer

Northwest, 59
Northeast, 72
Central, 93
South, 108
Everglades, 119

Float fishing, 38

Florida Game and Fresh Water Fish Commission

Regional office numbers, 19

Free-line, 5

G

Garfish, 15

J

Jigging, 7-8

K

Knots

Clinch knot, 39

L

Lakes

Alligator, 65
Bear, 51
Blue Cypress, 113
Brooklyn, 64
Bryant, 78
Butler, 78
Carlton, 76
Catherine, 114
Cherry, 67
Conway, 78
Crago, 98
Crescent, 76
Crooked, 98
Crosby, 63
Cypress, 79
Dead, 47
Deer Point, 44
Dexter, 82
Dora, 76
Dorr, 76
East Tohopekaliga, 80
Eustis, 77
Geneva, 64
George, 82
Griffin, 77

Lures

M

Management areas

FISHERMAN'S DIARY

FISH: _____

WEIGHT: _____

LENGTH: _____

WHEN: _____

WHERE: _____

BAIT USED: _____

NOTES: _____

_____

_____

_____

_____

FISH: _____

WEIGHT: _____

LENGTH: _____

WHEN: _____

WHERE: _____

BAIT USED: _____

NOTES: _____

_____

_____

_____

_____

_____

_____

_____

_____

_____

_____

FISH: _____

WEIGHT: _____

LENGTH: _____

WHEN: _____

WHERE: _____

BAIT USED: _____

NOTES: _____

_____

_____

_____

_____

_____

_____

_____

_____

_____

FISH: _____

WEIGHT: _____

LENGTH: _____

WHEN: _____

WHERE: _____

BAIT USED: _____

NOTES: _____

_____

_____

_____

_____

_____

_____

_____

_____

_____

FISH: _____

WEIGHT: _____

LENGTH: _____

WHEN: _____

WHERE: _____

BAIT USED: _____

NOTES: _____

_____

_____

_____

_____

_____

_____

_____

_____

_____

FISH:

WEIGHT:

LENGTH:

WHEN:

WHERE:

BAIT USED:

NOTES:

FISH:

WEIGHT:

LENGTH:

WHEN:

WHERE:

BAIT USED:

NOTES:

FISH: _____

WEIGHT: _____

LENGTH: _____

WHEN: _____

WHERE: _____

BAIT USED: _____

NOTES: _____

_____

_____

_____

_____

_____

_____

_____

_____

_____

FISH: _____

WEIGHT: _____

LENGTH: _____

WHEN: _____

WHERE: _____

BAIT USED: _____

NOTES: _____

_____

_____

_____

_____

_____

_____

_____

_____

_____

FISH: _____

WEIGHT: _____

LENGTH: _____

WHEN: _____

WHERE: _____

BAIT USED: _____

NOTES: _____

_____

_____

_____

_____

_____

_____

_____

_____

_____

_____

FISH:

WEIGHT:

LENGTH:

WHEN:

WHERE:

BAIT USED:

NOTES:

FISH: _____

WEIGHT: _____

LENGTH: _____

WHEN: _____

WHERE: _____

BAIT USED: _____

NOTES: _____

_____

_____

_____

_____

_____

_____

_____

_____

_____

OTHER BOOKS AND SPECIAL PUBLICATIONS OF THE ORLANDO SENTINEL

Quantity	Book	Mail price (out of state)	Mail price (Fla. residents, inc. 5% sales tax)
☐	Florida Home Grown: Landscaping By Tom MacCubbin	$8.95	$9.35
☐	The Florida Boating and Water Sports Guide By Max Branyon	$3.80	$3.95
☐	The Florida Gardening Guide	$3.35	$3.50
☐	Thought You'd Never Ask (Part I) By Dorothy Chapman	$9.95	$10.40
☐	Thought You'd Never Ask (Part II) By Dorothy Chapman	$9.95	$10.40
☐	Thought You'd Never Ask (Parts I and II) By Dorothy Chapman	$17.95	$18.75
☐	The Great Florida Adventure Catalog	$3.00	$3.00

Please send me the publications as indicated above. I enclose check or money order for the total Florida resident or out-of-state mail order price.

Please send my order to:

Name _____

Address _____

City _____

State _____ Zip Code _____